EAT HAPPY

MELISSA
HEMSLEY

The item should be returned or renewed by the last date stamped below.

Dylid dychwelyd neu adnewyddu'r eitem erbyn y dyddiad olaf sydd wedi'i stampio isod.

MALPAS

1 0 APR 2018

To renew visit / Adnewyddwch ar
www.newport.gov.uk/libraries

EAT HAPPY

MELISSA HEMSLEY

EBURY
PRESS

CONTENTS

INTRODUCTION

'**A**FTER spending a decade working in the food industry, the recipes that I and my family and friends come back to, time and time again, are those that are tasty, easy to cook, nourishing and thrifty. Eating well is for everyone and for every day. It can suit any budget and use ingredients from the corner shop down the road or foraged from the leftovers in your fridge or freezer. It can be straightforward to make, ready on the table in 30 minutes and, most importantly, it really can be delicious. '

In *Eat Happy* I want to bring the joy back to home cooking and show you how satisfying, affordable and quick food can be. These are fast, foolproof and fuss-free recipes that everyone will love and can tuck into any day of the week – simple dishes with big flavours using inexpensive, easy-to-get ingredients. No chef skills are required here; every recipe uses basic cooking techniques, with as few steps as possible and minimal washing-up, so that takeaways or ready meals never feel like the easier option.

One of the best tips my Mum taught me was how to respect food by not wasting it. She also taught me how to conjure up a meal out of very little and how to turn leftovers into meals that are actually delicious and you look forward to eating. This is always at the heart of my cooking. I'm happy to spend a bit of extra money on a few good-quality ingredients, such as well-sourced meat and dairy, but really, I'm a frugal shopper. I base my meals on foods stocked in my cupboard and freezer, along with fresh seasonal vegetables. I'm also a big fan of leftovers and won't ever waste food.

These recipes reflect this 'zero waste' approach. Instead of throwing away broccoli and herb stalks, they are incorporated into the dish and I give tips throughout the book for saving food to use later or for making tweaks to suit your needs. While most of the recipes serve four, they can easily be adapted for just one or two. And even if you cook the full amount, leftovers can be frozen or stored in the fridge to enjoy later in the week, so you cook less and enjoy more.

If you're cooking for the family, you'll notice lots of classic dishes that have been given a healthy twist but are full of familiar flavours that kids and grown-ups will both adore. A number of recipes take their cue from takeaways and ready meals. Well-loved favourites like pad Thai, burgers, pizza and curries are given a makeover by using whole food ingredients, with a few tricks here and there to keep them simple and yet tasting authentic. You'll find them more delicious, cheaper and quicker to make than it takes to order food in.

With these recipes, I also hope to inspire you to make the most of what you have in the fridge or freezer, rather than feeling obliged to pop out for a particular ingredient because you don't have it. In every recipe, I suggest different options for making the dish and ways to transform leftovers into a new meal to eat in or a delicious packed lunch to take out. With a bit of forward planning, you shouldn't need to go shopping more than once a week and you'll save money and time in the process.

The recipes in this book are not just about eating what's good for your body, they're also about enjoying and appreciating the food you put in your mouth. I hope you'll feel encouraged to have a go at combining nourishing ingredients in inventive and delicious ways, so that every day you can eat well and eat happy!

Making it work for you

The recipes here can all be cooked in 30 minutes and not only are they quick and enjoyable to make, but they use no more than two pans or baking trays. These recipes have been tested by my nearest and dearest, of all ages, abilities and patience levels, along with the harshest of critics, my godchildren, who now love to get involved and cook and this, in turn, has made them more adventurous with trying new green veg. I still can't train them to wash up, however, so it's a good thing that most of these recipes use only one pan!

Nifty cooking tips are included in the following pages and in the recipes to show you how to be more time efficient by using kitchen shortcuts and tricks; how to cook less by doubling up recipes and freezing and reusing leftovers; how to save money by reducing waste; and how to keep your kitchen well stocked to make life easier.
(See pp. 260 and 264 for more.)

I try to suggest ingredients that you can get locally or find in your fridge, freezer and cupboards. Throughout the recipes, I give ideas for adjusting them to suit different tastes and needs, along with variations and substitutions for swapping seasonal vegetables and other ingredients to keep things varied, exciting and cheaper.

Five top tips for using the recipes

- Double up and freeze. This is my number one tip for making life easier. Almost all of the recipes can be doubled and the second portion turned into another meal or a packed lunch.

- If you start a recipe and realise you haven't got everything, read the introduction and any Use It Up/Tips/Time Savers at the end of the recipe for suggestions and substitutions, or see p. 268 for simple swaps.

- Be inspired by the season. Use vegetables and herbs depending on what's on offer at your local shop or farmers' market, buy fish depending on what's the 'catch of the day', or make a delicious dinner based on what's in your fridge right now.

- I pack vegetables into recipes, but add more if you like, and enjoy a variety.

- Most recipes are complete meals, but elements can be mixed and matched with recipes in other chapters. In the recipes and chapter openers I've indicated what dishes will go with other ones in the book, but be bold and play around!

Cooking notes

TIMING
These recipes will take about 30 minutes based on using a preheated oven and with ingredients and equipment being ready to go. The timings are only approximate as we each cook at a different speed, ovens vary and distractions happen. Whatever the timing specified in a recipe, it is important to always check that meat and fish are cooked through.

REHEATING FOOD
Make sure your leftovers are heated right through leave a lid on the pan when reheating recipes like soup, porridge or stews to save time and not lose too much liquid or flavour. Don't boil but simmer on a low heat for as long as it takes for the dish to get hot all the way through.

QUALITY INGREDIENTS
I try to buy organic as much as possible, especially for animal products (meat, fish, eggs and dairy produce). Look for foods labelled 'organic', 'grass fed' and 'wild' (or 'sustainable' when it comes to fish) and if produce is unlabelled, don't be shy to ask questions of your suppliers. For fruit and veg where you eat the skin, or for produce with a large surface area, try to buy organic, particularly berries, apples, stone fruits, tomatoes and peppers, courgettes, salad leaves, leafy greens and fresh herbs. Organic coffee and cocoa beans are also worth seeking out as they are two of the most heavily sprayed crops.

SEASONAL & SWAPS
Try to eat with the seasons as much as possible, which also saves money. Variations appear in every recipe for substituting ingredients. See p. 268 for more last-minute swaps if you find yourself without a key ingredient.

LEFTOVERS & MINIMAL WASTE
Something my Mum taught me was to have two small containers out when cooking. Use the first for vegetable waste ready to empty into a larger recycling bin, along with any leftovers from dinner plates at the end of the day. Use a second container for odds and ends of leftover raw vegetables that you can pop straight into the fridge. This could be the second half of an onion, a peeled garlic clove you didn't end up using, the ends of some parsley stems, half a lemon. It's a shame to throw these odds and ends out. Every day I open the fridge and the container contents stare right at me, willing me to use them up! It's a friendly reminder to stop me wasting food and therefore money. (See p. 270 for more ways to make use of these ingredients.)

MEASUREMENTS
All spoon measures are level. For most measuring, you don't need to be exact and I like to use 'handfuls' to keep the cooking process more enjoyable, but when baking, do measure precisely.

OVEN TEMPERATURE
Recipes have been tested in a fan-assisted oven, so if you have a conventional oven set the temperature 20°C higher than the level stated in a recipe.

PORTION SIZES
In general, these recipes serve four people as a main dish, unless otherwise indicated.

SIZE & COLOUR
All fruit/veg are medium-sized unless otherwise stipulated. Use whatever colour you can get although if you have the option, go for a variety of colours.

READING LABELS

Take a few extra seconds to read labels, especially for added sugar or unrecognisable preservatives and flavourings, or if there are any allergies and intolerances to bear in mind.

COOKING MEAT

Fully defrost raw meat before cooking and always test to make sure chicken and pork are cooked through at the end of cooking. Pierce the meat with a sharp knife or skewer to make sure that the juices run clear.

MILK/YOGHURT

Use full-fat milk/yoghurt, whether dairy or non-dairy.

EGGS

These are medium-sized and should be used at room temperature. Note that in some recipes eggs are raw or partially cooked.

BUTTER

This is unsalted and at room temperature unless stated otherwise.

HERBS

Recipes indicate whether to use dried or fresh herbs, but either can be substituted: 1 teaspoon of dried herbs roughly equates with 1 tablespoon of the chopped fresh herb.

GHEE OR COCONUT OIL

I use these throughout but, if you prefer, use butter or olive oil.

CHILLI

The recipes are based on a medium strength of chilli, but feel free to adjust to your taste. You can substitute with any chilli you like – cayenne pepper, chilli powder/flakes or fresh chilli (p. 268) – but it's generally best to start with less and add more as you go, particularly if you're using fresh chillies, where the strength can be unpredictable.

BROTH/STOCK

Use bone broth or vegetable stock for tastier and more nourishing dishes. Either make your own (p. 278) or buy from a good source.

WASHING VEGETABLES

Always wash everything well, including rinsing dried foods like quinoa or buckwheat. Use a salad spinner for leafy greens and salad leaves to avoid soggy salads.

SOAKING

When you can, get into the habit of soaking uncooked legumes, quinoa, buckwheat and certain nuts and seeds. If you can't, rinse them well before cooking. (See p. 277 for more.)

CHOPPING

When chopping a large amount of onions, garlic, ginger or other vegetables (such as carrots, courgettes, peppers or cabbage), use a food processor to do it all for you. It can chop, shred and grate in seconds, as well as blend ingredients for dips and pesto. Or, use a spiralizer (p. 273) for slicing vegetables into strips.

Time-saving tips for 30-minute meals

TIME EFFICIENCY

I'm a big fan of prepping while other ingredients are cooking. If onions need to fry solo for 5 minutes, for instance, you've got 5 minutes to get on with chopping the garlic for cooking next. If a soup is left to simmer for 15 minutes, there's time to prepare any herb garnishes and toppings, or even get ahead and assemble a packed lunch or make a quick quinoa porridge (p. 18) for tomorrow's breakfast.

ROOM TEMPERATURE

Get meat and fish out of the fridge ahead of time. For speedy cooking, it's important for them to be at room temperature. Keep eggs and butter at room temperature.

PREHEAT THE OVEN

If you're baking and roasting, get that oven cranked up straight away as it needs a good 10–15 minutes to reach a high temperature. If you need to boil eggs or noodles, fill and boil the kettle in advance so that the water is just boiled and ready to go.

READ THROUGH & BE FLEXIBLE

Read a recipe through first and make sure you've got all the equipment and ingredients to hand. If you're missing certain ingredients, make decisions on what to use instead. Don't panic: just be flexible and use something else – there's almost always an alternative. (See p. 268 for some easy swaps.) When it comes to making curries and spicy dishes, a spice missed here or there is absolutely fine.

ESSENTIALS

Take 10 minutes to create an 'essentials' area, ideally near the stove. Mine has my all-rounder knife, a chopping board, and a couple of wooden spoons. Nearby sit the main seasonings – sea salt, black pepper and chilli flakes. Slightly away from the heat of the stove are the other flavouring essentials: extra-virgin olive oil, tamari, apple cider vinegar and, for frying and roasting, ghee and coconut oil.

A WIDE, DEEP PAN

Onions frying in a small saucepan will take longer to soften than in a large, wide pan, where they will be spread out in a single layer and cook more quickly. The same applies to roasting in the oven. If your meat and vegetables are on top of each other in a small dish, they'll cook slowly and steam rather than roast. For fast cooking, spread them out in a single layer in the largest baking tray you can fit in your oven.

LINING BAKING TRAYS

When you are cooking a dish with lots of sticky sauce, line your baking tray(s) with baking parchment to make the clean-up process easier.

RELAX & ENJOY!

The timings given are just a guide. If time isn't pressing, take more time over things and enjoy the process. Spending time at the end to taste for seasoning, adjusting with a little salt, pepper and a squeeze of lemon or lime to bring out flavours, can make all the difference to a dish. This book is called *Eat Happy*, after all!

BREAKFAST & BRUNCH

'WHEREVER the day takes you, start it off in the right way with a delicious and healthy breakfast in your belly. We're all in a rush in the morning but don't miss out on breakfast, because it will jump-start your day and give you sustained energy through to lunch.'

There are lots of ways to liven up your breakfast without needing to stand in front of a stove, and you don't need to come up with something different every day. If you don't feel like food first thing in the morning, or don't have the time to eat it before leaving home, try one of the portable breakfasts here and enjoy it when you get to work. Recipes like the Easy Granola (p. 22), Spinach & Smoked Trout Muffins (p. 25) and Perfect Pancakes (p. 36) can be made the night before, or earlier in the week, and grabbed to go.

Don't feel you have to eat a particular sort of food at a particular time of day. I enjoy leftover soup for breakfast – such as the Ginger Miso Sunshine Soup (p. 59) – and I'd be equally happy with the Turkish Scrambled Eggs (p. 29) for supper, so don't just stick to the recipes in this chapter. It's also great to enjoy a variety of foods so even when you've got your favourites, every month try something new.

At the same time, there is nothing like having a few faithful standbys up your sleeve. For many of us, breakfast tends to revolve around bread, mainly because it's delicious, convenient and means you don't have to think too much first thing in the morning. Quick Quinoa Bread (p. 21) is a 30-minute loaf that's a real hunger-buster as it's high in protein and nutrient-rich. No baking skills are needed, you can make it ahead of time, freeze in slices and toast from frozen and enjoy with a range of toppings. Eggs are a wonderfully convenient food too, of course, and they are included in many of the recipes here. As well as being full of protein and good fat, they go with everything, they're quick to cook and you can't really go wrong – even if you overcook a yolk, it's still delicious.

If you're looking to sneak in an extra portion of vegetables whenever you can, breakfast should be no exception. You'll see that almost every recipe in this chapter has some greens in it. The quickest vegetables to prepare are the leafy greens, which barely need to be cooked: spinach takes only a minute, while kale, chard and spring greens take just a few minutes more. Cabbage in all its different varieties is one of my favourites – cheap and cheerful and it goes perfectly with an egg! I really recommend the Indian-Spiced Cabbage Scramble (p. 30).

Follow the Japanese and Scandinavian lead and try some oily fish for breakfast; they are so good for you. You'll see that I use smoked trout in muffins (p. 25) and spread mackerel pâté on toast (p. 24) and salmon in NYC-style Big Blinis (p. 38). Take a look at the Sardine Fishcakes, too, from the 'Fish' chapter (p. 106). One of these for brunch with a poached egg would be delicious.

For more breakfast ideas try:

Any Time Blueberry Bake
    Sweets (p. 214)

Carrot Fritters
    Sides (p. 200)

Ginger, Fruit & Nut Muffins
    Sweets (p. 238)

Green Go-getter Smoothie
    Drinks (p. 252)

Turkish Wraps with Spinach & Feta
    Vegetable Mains (p. 144)

Roasted Fruit with Cardamom & Ginger Yoghurt
    Sweet (p. 239)

Sardine Fish Cakes
    Fish (p. 116)

Quinoa power porridge

Choose from three different quinoa options and play around with flavours. There are seven here, one for every day of the week! I'm a fan of porridge in a flask for an easy warming breakfast on the go. If I have people over, I make a huge pan of porridge and put small bowls out with a selection of flavours and toppings to let everyone help themselves.

Serves 2

400–500ml any milk
500ml hot water
2 teaspoons coconut oil
   or butter
1 teaspoon vanilla extract
2 teaspoons maple syrup or
   raw honey (optional)

QUINOA OPTIONS
200g quinoa flakes
250g cooked quinoa (p. 150)
100g uncooked quinoa, rinsed
   well (ideally soaked first,
   p. 277)

Quinoa flakes: Toast the quinoa flakes in a dry pan on a medium heat for 1 minute, stirring frequently to prevent them from burning. This reduces any bitterness and gives a nice nutty flavour. Add 400ml of milk and all the other ingredients, give everything a stir and bring to a medium simmer. Cook for 4 minutes, then add your choice of flavourings.

Cooked quinoa: Place the cooked quinoa in a saucepan, add 400ml of milk and all the other ingredients. Bring to a medium simmer and cook for 4 minutes, then add your choice of flavourings.

Uncooked quinoa: Place the uncooked quinoa in a saucepan, add 500ml of milk and all the other ingredients. Bring to a medium simmer and cook, covered, until the liquid has been absorbed and the quinoa is tender, about 15 minutes (or 12 minutes if the quinoa has been soaked), then add your choice of flavourings.

FLAVOURING OPTIONS
If you need to toast any nuts or seeds, dry-toast them in the pan first, on a medium heat for a minute or so, then set aside before you add the quinoa. This avoids using more than one pan.

Berries & toasted almonds: Top with 1 tablespoon of toasted flaked or chopped almonds and a handful of berries. (Frozen berries can be stirred through hot porridge.)

Fig, pistachio & pomegranate: Top with 1 sliced large ripe fig, 1 tablespoon of pistachios, 1 tablespoon of pomegranate seeds and a drizzle of raw honey.

Tropical medley: Top with 2 tablespoons of (toasted) coconut flakes, 1 chopped kiwi fruit, or a little chopped papaya, plus a squeeze of lime juice over the fruit.

Spiced & creamy: At the end of cooking, stir through 1 tablespoon of nut or seed butter (p. 276), 1 teaspoon of ground cinnamon, ½ teaspoon of ground turmeric and 1 tablespoon of dried cranberries or goji berries.

Pear, pecan & ginger: Stir in 2 teaspoons of grated ginger and ½ teaspoon of ground cinnamon, and top with 1 sliced large ripe pear and 1 tablespoon of roughly chopped pecans.

Chocolate & hazelnut: Stir in 2 tablespoons of cocoa powder and top with 2 tablespoons of roughly chopped toasted hazelnuts.

Açai & banana: Stir in 1½ tablespoons of açai berry powder or frozen acai berries and top with some sliced banana and a little lime juice and zest.

'Apple pie' buckwheat porridge

Buckwheat groats offer a good alternative to regular rolled oats, making a hearty bowl of porridge that will keep you satisfied until lunch. The natural nuttiness of buckwheat goes particularly well with 'apple pie' flavours like vanilla, cinnamon and maple syrup. Bear in mind that buckwheat tends to soak up a lot of flavour so I generally increase my normal amount of spices and additions to make sure it's delicious. For extra creaminess, stir through a tablespoon of almond or other nut butter before serving. Or you could serve this with one of the seven different flavouring options for Quinoa Power Porridge (p. 18). Make a big panful, if you prefer, and then just heat through individual portions during the week with an extra splash of water. For a portable breakfast, you could pour the hot porridge into a vacuum flask to enjoy later.

Serves 4

200g buckwheat groats, rinsed
   well (ideally soaked first,
   p. 277)
700ml any milk
1 large handful of sultanas
   or currants
4 apples (such as Cox or
   Braeburn), grated
1½ tablespoon butter or
   coconut oil
2 teaspoons vanilla extract
1 tablespoon ground
   cinnamon, plus extra
   to serve
A small pinch of sea salt
Maple syrup or raw honey
   (or to taste)
4 tablespoons flaked almonds,
   to serve

1. Sprinkle the almonds (to serve) in a large, wide pan and dry-toast for a minute or so over a medium heat, tossing occasionally to make sure they don't burn, then set aside.

2. Place the same pan back on the hob, add the buckwheat and cook over a medium-high heat for a few minutes, stirring occasionally, for the liquid to evaporate and for the groats to get lightly toasted to bring out their nutty flavour.

3. Pour the milk into the pan and cover with a lid. Bring to the boil, then reduce the heat to medium and simmer for 18 minutes (or 15 minutes if the buckwheat has been soaked) until cooked.

4. Halfway through the cooking time, stir in half the grated apple with the butter, vanilla extract, cinnamon and salt.

5. Sweeten to taste with maple syrup or honey and serve sprinkled with the remaining grated apple, an extra dusting of cinnamon and the toasted almonds.

✳ Use It Up

Swap two of the apples for two carrots that need using up for a 'carrot cake' flavour! Sprinkle over a handful of fresh berries – blueberries, raspberries or blackberries – to serve if you have any leftover in the fridge.

Quick quinoa bread

Simple to make, with no baking skills required, this nutrient-rich loaf of bread is ready in just half an hour! This bread freezes well, so you could slice it up to have whenever you want it and either defrost or toast individual slices straight from frozen in the oven. My favourite way to have it is toasted for 40 seconds on each side in a hot dry frying pan or griddle pan. It tastes best with savoury toppings: fried egg and bacon, garlic mushrooms, roasted cherry tomatoes with basil. Eaten fresh, it makes a great sandwich or you can just serve it buttered with a bowl of soup. Quinoa flour and buttermilk are widely available, though you can easily make buttermilk yourself - simply mix 150ml of dairy or nut/seed milk (p. 276) with 1 tablespoon of lemon juice or apple cider vinegar. Leave to stand for 12–15 minutes to curdle into buttermilk.

Makes 1 small loaf (12 slices)

Butter or coconut oil,
   for greasing
200g quinoa flour
1 teaspoon bicarbonate of soda
½ teaspoon sea salt
1 teaspoon dried herbs (such
   as thyme or rosemary)
1 egg
165ml buttermilk (or make
   your own)
1 tablespoon maple syrup
1 handful of mixed seeds
   (pumpkin, sunflower or
   sesame seeds)

1. Preheat the oven to fan 190°C/Gas mark 6½ and grease an 8cm x 18cm loaf tin with butter.

2. In a large bowl, mix the quinoa flour with the bicarbonate of soda, salt and herbs.

3. Make a hole in the middle, crack in the egg and whisk it, then add the buttermilk and maple syrup. Stir until combined, then pour the mixture into the prepared tin, spreading it out evenly. Sprinkle with mixed seeds, if using.

4. Bake in the oven for 20–22 minutes until golden brown and a skewer inserted into the middle of the loaf comes out clean. Allow to cool in the tin for a few minutes, then remove from the tin and transfer to a wire rack. Once the loaf has cooled, you can cut it into slices about 1cm thick.

✳ Use It Up

Swap the dried herbs for 1 tablespoon of chopped fresh herbs. For a focaccia-style loaf, chop up two sun-dried tomatoes or pitted olives and add to the batter with a finely chopped clove of garlic.

Easy granola

The ingredients in this recipe are relatively expensive but worth it as granola is perfect for breakfast or a snack. It lasts for about two weeks in an airtight container and would make a great gift too. As granola is so portable, I like to eat a cooked breakfast at home and save granola for the mornings when I need something 'to go'. Use an empty jar and layer the granola with yoghurt and some fresh berries or roasted fruit (p. 239), or grate over some apple or even carrot! You can play around with spices as well: ground cinnamon adds a natural sweetness, but you could swap it for ground cardamom, ginger or nutmeg.

Makes 1.5kg granola (12–14 portions)

250g quinoa or buckwheat flakes
5 tablespoons coconut oil
3 tablespoons maple syrup
2 teaspoons vanilla extract
1 tablespoon ground cinnamon
A pinch of sea salt
200g coconut flakes
200g mixed dried fruit (such as cranberries, raisins, apricots or chopped dates)

NUTS AND SEEDS
400g mixed nuts (such as pecans, hazelnuts or Brazil nuts)
400g mixed seeds (such as pumpkin, sunflower or sesame seeds)

1. Preheat the oven to fan 160°C/Gas mark 4.

2. Place the mixed nuts in a food processor and pulse briefly so they are roughly chopped. Add to a large bowl with the quinoa or buckwheat flakes and the mixed seeds.

3. In a small pan, gently warm through the coconut oil, maple syrup, vanilla extract, cinnamon and salt until the coconut oil has melted. Pour into the bowl and stir in to coat the nut mixture.

4. Spread out on two large baking trays and bake in the oven for 20 minutes until just golden brown. Toss halfway through cooking and add the coconut flakes.

5. Remove from the oven and pour back into the bowl. Mix in the dried fruit and, once cooled, transfer to a big jar (sterilised first, p. 267) or an airtight container.

Chocolate orange granola

Make the granola as above, then, once cooled, stir through the zest of 1 orange and 60g of dark chocolate chips. To make chocolate chips yourself, carefully chop up 60g of dark (70%–85%) chocolate with a sharp knife, or break into squares and pulse in a food processor. This granola would be perfect as a Christmas present or for a special breakfast. It would also be delicious served as a crunchy topping for warm poached pears.

Smoked mackerel pâté

Mackerel pâté might not be the first thing that springs to mind for breakfast, but just think of it as another version of a smoked salmon and cream cheese bagel! It's really tasty with smoked trout too. The pâté is simple – just blend the ingredients, spread on the toast and, if you like, top with some raw fresh vegetables cut into wafer-thin slices. It's also extremely versatile: enjoy as a snack with crudités or Chickpea Crackers (p. 212), or, for quick canapés, spoon onto rings made from crunchy vegetables, such as multicoloured beetroots, cucumber, daikon radishes or serve some on the blinis from page 218.

Serves 4

SMOKED MACKEREL PÂTÉ
3 smoked mackerel fillets
   (total 200g), skin removed
200g cream cheese
Juice of ½ lemon, plus extra
   to serve
1–2 teaspoons mustard
   (or to taste – optional)
1 small handful of fresh dill or
   parsley, roughly chopped,
   plus extra to serve
Sea salt and black pepper

TO SERVE (OPTIONAL)
Quick Quinoa Bread (p. 21)
Thinly shaved slices of
   cucumber, raw beetroot or
   red onion
2 large handfuls of watercress
   or salad leaves

1. Place all the ingredients for the pâté in a food processor, season with salt and pepper and blend. Alternatively, add everything to a large bowl and mix with a fork.

2. Taste for seasoning, adding a little more lemon juice, if you like. Spoon into a serving dish and sprinkle over some extra pepper and chopped herbs.

3. To serve, toast some bread and top with the mackerel pâté, allowing two slices of toast per person. Squeeze over some extra lemon juice, season to taste with salt and pepper and add a few slices of cucumber, beetroot, red onion, watercress or salad leaves.

✱ Use It Up

Replace the mustard with wasabi or horseradish.

Spinach & smoked trout muffins

Muffins make the perfect portable breakfast: they cook quickly and are easy to 'grab and go'. This smoked trout version is a great way to eat more omega-3-rich fish; you can swap the trout for smoked salmon or mackerel, if you prefer. Baby spinach works well here as it needs no precooking. Delicious warm or cold.

Makes 12 muffins

Butter or coconut oil, for
   greasing (optional)
8 eggs
100g smoked trout, skin
   removed and flesh
   roughly flaked
150g baby spinach, scrunched
   up and roughly chopped
4 spring onions, sliced
1 small handful of fresh basil,
   chopped
½ teaspoon sea salt
¼ teaspoon black pepper

1. Preheat the oven to fan 190°C/Gas mark 6½ and pop a paper case into each hole of a 12-hole muffin tin. Alternatively, grease the tin well with butter if you don't have any muffin cases.

2. In a large bowl, beat the eggs and then mix in all the other ingredients.

3. Divide the batter among the muffin cases and bake in the oven for 10–12 minutes until set in the middle (if you insert a toothpick or skewer into a muffin, it should come out clean).

4. Allow to cool in the tin for a few minutes before transferring to a wire rack. Enjoy warm, or grab and go to eat later. They last about three days if kept in the fridge.

Spinach & smoked trout frittata

Turn this mixture into a frittata for an easy lunch party. Melt 1 tablespoon of butter or coconut oil in a large frying pan, then pour in the batter and cook, covered, over a medium heat for about 8 minutes until set on the bottom. Remove the lid and grill on a high heat for 4–6 minutes until set in the middle. Add a handful of any leftover grated cheese on top for that golden finish. Allow to cool for 5 minutes, then transfer to a board and slice into thick wedges to serve.

✳ Use It Up

If you have some chard or kale to use up, chop it up very finely before adding to the batter as it will otewise need longer to cook. Play around with flavours: swap the basil for parsley or dill, or if you don't have fresh herbs, use 1 teaspoon of dried herbs such as thyme or oregano.

Pizza omelette

This is great for a solo breakfast or a 10-minute supper and it travels well, too. If you have any leftover veg that needs eating – a bit of broccoli, the end of a courgette, half a pepper – chop it up and add to the mushrooms as they fry. Use a wide, ovenproof pan, so that the pizza omelette is thin and therefore sets in just a few minutes. Serve with a pile of rocket, or any leaves, dressed with lemon juice and olive oil.

Serves 1

2 teaspoons butter or ghee
2 garlic cloves, finely chopped
150 g mushrooms, sliced
1 teaspoon dried herbs (such
 as oregano or thyme)
3 eggs
4 cherry tomatoes, halved
1 handful of grated Parmesan
Sea salt and black pepper

OPTIONAL EXTRAS
Pitted olives
Tinned anchovies
Cured ham slices
Sun-dried tomatoes, chopped
Roasted red peppers, chopped
Capers

TO SERVE
Chilli flakes
Fresh basil leaves
1 very large handful of rocket
A squeeze of lemon juice
Extra-virgin olive oil

1. Preheat the grill to high and melt the butter in an 18cm ovenproof frying pan. Add the garlic and fry for 30 seconds, then add the mushrooms and herbs and cook over a medium heat for 4 minutes or until the mushrooms have released their liquid and are turning golden.

2. Meanwhile, whisk the eggs together with some salt and pepper, then pour into the pan, tipping it from side to side so that the egg coats the bottom in an even layer. Add the tomatoes, skin side down, and any optional extras, spacing them out evenly.

3. After a few minutes, the bottom of the omelette will be set and lightly browned. Make sure the heat isn't too high, so the omelette doesn't burn.

4. Scatter the cheese on top and pop under the hot grill for 2–3 minutes until the eggs are cooked through and the cheese is golden, then gently tip the omelette onto your plate.

5. Top with some chilli flakes and fresh basil leaves. Add the rocket on the side, dress with lemon juice and olive oil and serve immediately.

✳ Use It Up

Swap the Parmesan for grated mature Cheddar or tear up some mozzarella. Alternatively, use up whatever cheese you have leftover in the fridge.

Turkish scrambled eggs

If you love *shakshuka* or *huevos rancheros*, then this Turkish dish of softly scrambled egg (*menemen*) is going to be your new favourite. It has the added bonus of being a one-pan dish, as you crack the eggs straight into the pan without needing to whisk them first in a separate bowl. Look out for Aleppo chilli flakes – known in Turkey as *pul biber* – for an authentic touch. Serve with toast, warmed Chickpea Wraps (p. 190) or Buckwheat Naans (p. 191), and a handful of parsley leaves. Enjoy with a fresh mint tea (p. 257), as pictured here.

Serves 2

1 tablespoon butter or ghee
1 small onion, finely chopped
1 red pepper,
   deseeded and diced
1 handful of fresh parsley,
   stalks finely chopped and
   leaves roughly chopped
1 garlic clove, finely chopped
½–1 teaspoon chilli flakes
   (to taste), plus extra to serve
2 tomatoes, diced, or 100g
   cherry tomatoes, quartered
4 eggs
Sea salt and black pepper

TO SERVE
1 handful of feta, crumbled
Extra-virgin olive oil

1. Melt the butter in a wide frying pan, add the onion, pepper, parsley stalks, garlic and chilli flakes and fry on a medium heat for 5 minutes to soften, stirring occasionally.

2. Add the tomatoes then increase the heat and fry for a further 5 minutes.

3. Turn the heat down to low and push the cooked vegetables to one side. Crack the eggs into the space left in the pan and use a wooden spoon to mix the yolks into the whites for about 20 seconds, seasoning with a little salt and pepper. Gently stir the cooked vegetables into the eggs for about 1 minute until the eggs are just cooked but still soft and a bit runny. Immediately remove from the heat (remember that the eggs will continue to cook in the pan).

4. Sprinkle over the parsley leaves and feta (if using), drizzle over the olive oil, add a sprinkle of extra chilli and serve straight away.

Indian-spiced cabbage scramble

Yes, cabbage for breakfast! Served with your favourite Indian spices and some softly scrambled eggs. This is my kind of fast food for any time of day – the ingredients are cheap and you can get them everywhere. Any kind of cabbage will work here – white, green or red. Serve on toast, in a Chickpea Wrap (p. 190), on a Buckwheat Naan (p. 191), or with some cooked red lentils or quinoa.

Serves 4

1 tablespoon butter or ghee
½ red onion, finely chopped
1 fresh chilli, deseeded and finely chopped (or to taste)
8mm of ginger, finely chopped
½ teaspoon ground turmeric
1 small handful of fresh coriander, stalks finely chopped and leaves roughly chopped
1 small cabbage (about 300g), leaves cut into 4mm slices
1 large tomato, diced
8 eggs
Sea salt and black pepper

1. Melt the butter in a wide frying pan, add the onion, chilli, ginger, turmeric and coriander stalks and fry together over a medium heat for just under a minute, stirring occasionally.

2. Add the cabbage and tomatoes and stir-fry for 3–4 minutes until the cabbage has softened. Add a splash of water if the mixture starts to stick.

3. Push everything to the side of the pan, reduce the heat to low and crack the eggs into the empty space. Immediately start to gently scramble the eggs with a wooden spoon for about 30 seconds to mix the yolks and whites. Season the eggs with salt and pepper and then stir everything together so that the eggs gently cook in the rest of the mixture.

4. Remove from the heat and serve immediately, sprinkled with the chopped coriander leaves.

Harissa greens with eggs & feta

A delicious way to eat more dark leafy greens at breakfast. Harissa, whether it's powder or paste, adds such a big hit of instant flavour to any dish and it's available everywhere now, but you could add your own favourite spice if you prefer – chilli and cumin or a bit of sweet smoked paprika. You could swap the cheese for smoked trout or salmon, if you prefer, adding it at the end to serve. I like to finish this under a hot grill, but you can cook the eggs on the hob for three to five minutes, covered with a lid, until the whites have set and the yolks are done just to your liking.

Serves 2

1½ tablespoons coconut oil
   or ghee
1 teaspoon harissa powder or
   1 tablespoon harissa paste
150g spinach
4 eggs
40g feta or goat's cheese,
   crumbled
Sea salt and black pepper
½ lemon, cut into wedges,
   to serve

1. Preheat the grill to high.

2. Melt the coconut oil in a large, wide pan over a medium-high heat and stir in the harissa.

3. Stir in the spinach and put a lid on the pan to cook for 2 minutes until they have started to wilt. Use a wooden spoon to make four gaps in the greens and crack an egg into each gap.

4. Sprinkle a little salt and pepper over everything, dot the cheese around the greens and pop under the grill to cook for 3–4 minutes until the whites have set, the yolks are still runny and the cheese is melted. Alternatively, add the cheese at the end if you want it cool and creamy. Serve with a wedge of lemon.

✳ Use It Up

You can also use chard or kale instead of spinach. Simply slice the leaves into ribbons and cook for 3-4 minutes in step 2 of the method.

Fried eggs, avocado & smoky bean tacos

Fried eggs go perfectly here, but if you're making this for more than two people, scrambled eggs are best as they are much quicker and easier to do for a group. The Chickpea Wraps (p.190) are super fast to make so start with these and enjoy the leftover wraps for packed lunches during the week.

Serves 2

4 Chickpea Wraps (p. 190)
1 tablespoon butter or ghee
1 teaspoon smoked paprika
1 tablespoon tomato purée
1 x 400g tin of beans, drained
 and rinsed
Flesh of 1 avocado, thinly
 sliced
4 eggs
½ quantity of Jalapeño Salsa
 (p. 113)
Sea salt and black pepper

TO SERVE
1 small handful of fresh
 coriander leaves,
 roughly torn
1 fresh red chilli, deseeded and
 sliced (to taste)

1. Lay two chickpea wraps on each plate so they are overlapping slightly.

2. Heat a wide frying pan to high, add half the butter, the smoked paprika and tomato purée and fry over a medium heat for 1 minute before stirring in the beans. Heat through for 2–3 minutes, then season with salt and pepper to taste and divide among the chickpea wraps. Lay the sliced avocado on top.

3. Wipe the pan clean with kitchen paper and melt the remaining butter. When the butter has melted, crack in the eggs and cook over a medium-high heat for 3–4 minutes until the whites are becoming crisp around the edges but the yolks are still runny. Season with salt and pepper to taste, then add an egg to each of the wraps and drizzle over the salsa. Serve sprinkled with the fresh coriander and chilli.

✳ Use It Up

You can use any type of beans, tinned or cooked (p. 271), or swap the smoky beans for leftover Spiced Beans (p. 35).

Smoked mackerel & jalapeño salsa tacos

These are made with roughly flaked smoked mackerel, but use any cooked fish you like.

Serves 2

4 Chickpea Wraps (p. 190)
2 handfuls of watercress
2 tomatoes, choppped
2 smoked mackerel fillets
2 spring onions, sliced
½ quantity of Jalapeño Salsa
 (p. 113)

1. Lay two chickpea wraps on each plate.

2. Divide the watercress between the wraps, add the tomatoes, top with the flaked fish and spring onions then drizzle over the salsa.

Spiced beans & halloumi

These homemade beans are lightly spiced with a lovely thick sauce. Any leftovers of these spiced beans are perfect in a Waste Not, Want Not Bowl (p. 72), so I always make extra to keep in the fridge. You could serve them with a fried or poached egg on top, but they are especially tasty with fried halloumi. Look for good-quality halloumi and keep a few packets in the fridge; it lasts well and is ideal for adding a special touch to a simple meal.

Serves 4

8 slices of Quick Quinoa Bread
    (p. 21), or your choice of
bread
1 teaspoon coconut oil or ghee
250g halloumi cheese, cut into
    1cm cubes

BEANS
1 tablespoon coconut oil
    or ghee
1 onion, finely chopped
2 garlic cloves, finely chopped
½ teaspoon smoked paprika
A pinch of chilli flakes
1 tablespoon tomato purée
1 x 400g tin of chopped
    tomatoes
1 tablespoon maple syrup
½ tablespoon apple cider
    vinegar
2 x 400g tins of haricot beans,
    drained and rinsed
Sea salt and black pepper

1. First make the beans. Melt the oil in a wide frying pan, add the onion and fry over a medium heat for 5 minutes until softened, then add the garlic and spices and cook for another minute.

2. Stir in the tomato purée and fry for 30 seconds. Add the tinned tomatoes, maple syrup and apple cider vinegar and season with salt and pepper. Bring to the boil, then reduce to a medium heat and simmer for 5 minutes, uncovered tip in the beans and continue to simmer for a further 5 minutes until cooked through with a thick sauce. Season to taste.

3. Meanwhile, toast the quinoa bread (if using) in a dry pan over a medium-high heat for about 40 seconds on each side, then add two slices to each plate.

4. A few minutes before the beans are ready, melt the remaining oil in the second pan and fry the halloumi pieces over a high heat for a couple of minutes, tossing occasionally, until golden brown.

5. Divide the beans among the plates, then cover each portion with the fried halloumi and serve immediately.

✳ Use It Up

Any beans or chickpeas work well here. Try with any leftover cheese: feta, crumbled goat's cheese, or that last bit of grated Cheddar.

Perfect pancakes

Although made with bananas, these pancakes don't taste strongly of them. Banana is used to give substance and a natural sweetness, while the quinoa flakes and egg not only add protein but also help bind the mixture. I make these about 1cm thick and very rustically shaped, but if you've got a pancake ring, whip it out to make a pretty stack. If you want to double the recipe (especially if you have bananas that need using up), any extra pancakes will keep in the fridge for a few days, or you can freeze them. Pop them in the oven or fry in a pan to reheat.

Serves 2 / makes 8 pancakes

2 ripe bananas (total 200g), peeled
100g quinoa flakes
180ml any milk
1 egg
1 teaspoon vanilla extract
2 teaspoons ground cinnamon
1½ teaspoons baking powder
A tiny pinch of sea salt
2 teaspoons maple syrup
1½–2 tablespoons coconut oil, for frying

TOPPING OPTIONS

100g mixed berries, a spoonful of natural yoghurt, crushed pistachios and a drizzle of maple syrup
2 apples, grated, a sprinkling of cinnamon and a spoonful of toasted flaked almonds

1. Place all the ingredients for the pancakes (except the oil) in a blender or food processor and whizz for about 30 seconds. Alternatively, mash the bananas with a fork and mix in a jug with all the remaining ingredients.

2. Melt a little of the coconut oil in a large frying pan on a high heat.

3. Spoon about 3 tablespoons of the batter into the pan and use the back of the spoon to swirl into a rough circle about 1cm thick and 8cm wide. Repeat to make another two to three pancakes, depending on the size of your pan. Reduce the heat to medium and leave the pancakes to set for 1½ minutes. When they start to bubble, flip each one over and cook for 1 minute on the other side.

4. Remove from the pan and repeat with the rest of the batter, using a little more of the coconut oil each time, until you have made eight pancakes. Place the pancakes on a plate in a low oven to keep warm while you make the rest.

5. Serve as is or add your favourite toppings.

✳ Use It Up

This recipe is ideal for when you have a bowl of really ripe bananas that need using up!

NYC-style big blinis

These are a must make! A fusion of a blini and a bagel, they are really easy to prepare. You could make a load in advance, then freeze and reheat them, or make them from scratch in just 15 minutes. Always serve them with a generous smear of cream cheese and add fillings. Try this New York-style filling, with smoked salmon, cucumber and capers, or a veggie version with avocado, red onion and slices of roasted or fresh red pepper. They would also be great with scrambled eggs and bacon. See p. 218 for smaller, bite-sized blinis served as party canapés.

Serves 4

BUCKWHEAT BLINIS
1 egg
85g buckwheat flour
1 teaspoon baking powder
125ml any milk
2 tablespoons butter or ghee
Sea salt and black pepper

SMOKED SALMON
100g smoked salmon slices
½ cucumber, thinly sliced
2 tablespoons capers
½ red onion, thinly sliced
1 large handful of watercress,
    rocket or baby spinach
200g full-fat cream cheese,
    to serve
½ lemon, cut into wedges,
    to serve

1. Whisk the egg in a large jug, then add flour, baking powder, ¼ teaspoon each of salt and pepper and a splash of the milk and mix into a thick paste. Slowly mix in the rest of the milk (adding it gradually will prevent the mixture from becoming lumpy). You can also make the batter in advance (just keep it in the fridge overnight), and whisk again before serving.

2. Heat a large frying pan – wide enough to fry two blinis at a time – and add the butter. When the butter has melted, pour any excess into a small jug. Pour out enough batter (about 1½ tablespoons) to form a circle on one side of the pan. Use the back of the spoon to shape the batter into an even shape, 6cm wide and 5mm thick, then pour out another circle of batter on the other side of the pan.

3. Cook on a medium heat for 1½ minutes, then flip over and cook on the other side for another 1½ minutes until just golden brown. Remove from the pan and leave to cool, then repeat with the rest of the batter, using more melted butter as needed, until you have eight blinis.

4. Spread four of the blinis with a generous helping of cream cheese and layer up with smoked salmon, cucumber, capers, red onion and watercress. Season with a little salt and pepper and sandwich together with the remaining four blinis. Serve with a wedge of lemon to squeeze over.

Birthday breakfast

My friend and chief recipe tester, Kitty, made a giant pan of this the morning after her birthday, so I always think of it as a birthday breakfast, but it will do nicely for any breakfast or indeed any meal of the day. It is an excellent way of using up any greens you have languishing in the fridge, not just spinach, and any cheese goes. All the action happens in the oven; you just need to crack the eggs into the dish and pop it back into the oven just before you're ready to eat. Serve with Quinoa Bread (p. 21) and some guacamole (p.53), or just a green juice (p.252) as pictured here.

Serves 4

1½ tablespoons coconut oil or ghee
Flesh of 1 butternut squash (about 1kg), cut into 1cm cubes
200g cherry tomatoes
200g spinach
4-8 eggs (depending on the size of your pan, and how hungry you are!)
1 teaspoon chilli flakes
60g mature Cheddar, grated
Sea salt and black pepper

1. Preheat the oven to fan 220°C/Gas mark 9. Put the oil into a very large ovenproof dish or roasting tin and place in the oven for a few minutes for the oil to melt, then carefully remove. Use two trays if you need to, especially if you're making extra eggs.

2. Toss the squash and cherry tomatoes in the melted oil and roast in the oven for 18 minutes. Remove the dish, tossing everything together, add the spinach and return to the oven.

3. After 5 minutes, the spinach will have wilted, so remove the dish again and nudge things around with a wooden spoon to create four to eight small gaps. Crack in the eggs, season with salt, pepper and chilli flakes, scatter over the cheese and return to the oven for another 2–3 minutes until the whites have just set and yolks are still runny.

BOWL FOOD

' THE biggest chapter in the book, 'Bowl Food' features soups, stews and curries – anything comforting and with a sauce. Here you'll find a range of different ways to fill a bowl with delicious and nourishing food without breaking a sweat, and you'll find that bowls are the perfect vessel for leftovers. '

Soups are the ultimate easy and simple meal – affordable, flexible and portable. These supercharged soup recipes are hearty, full of goodness and satisfying, not to mention really easy to make and digest. Try the Monday Miso Noodle Soup (p. 46), for instance, or the Tuscan Bean Soup with Parmesan Bites (p. 60) – each a meal in themselves. And if you haven't already, spend a bit of time finding your best source of good-quality stock or broth – unless you plan to make your own (p. 278). A good stock or broth adds extra flavour and is what makes a dish feel really satisfying.

The definition of a stew is a dish simmered over a low heat, that's not too wet, simmered over a low heat. However, in the spirit of fast food, I've taken the bits I like from my favourite stews and turned them into something between a soup and stew, all in 30 minutes. Of course, if you have a little more time, just let them gently simmer away for longer. Try the wonderfully comforting Sausage Stew (p. 61) or the delicious tagine on p. 54.

Soups and stews are so flexible because you can mix and match your vegetables, lentils and beans, spices and herbs as much as you like, making it either broth-like or thicker and richer. If you've only got 30 minutes to cook for the whole week, make a soup or stew. Something like the Greek Red Lentil Soup (p. 48) or the Ginger & Miso Sunshine Soup (p. 59) will take you less than 30 minutes and you can make double the recipe to give you enough to eat throughout the week. Use it as a base and top it or pair it with other ingredients to add variety. Try filling up an insulated flask for a warming lunch on the go.

One of the great things about bowl food is that you can get away with things being a little 'rustic', so you can afford to be casual, even a bit lazy, about the way you chop things, especially if you're going to blend them up to be silky smooth. But if you're having people over or just want to make a bit more effort for yourself, then it's important to have some finishing touches to hand. Do have a go at the ones included here, such as the tasty gremolata for adding to the lentil stew on p. 49 or the Parmesan bites for serving with the Tuscan Bean Soup (p. 60).

Even just a few chopped herbs, a drizzle of olive oil or a few toasted chopped nuts can be all that's needed to bring out the flavours in a dish. You'll find suggestions throughout the recipes and feel free to mix and match from one dish to another. And there is always room for extra greens! Stir fresh spinach through a soup or stew to wilt in a minute, top with shredded cabbage or a slaw (p. 177), or just serve up your hot bowls and add a big handful of rocket or watercress on top. You can feel it doing you good and it's so tasty too!

For more food that's good to eat in a bowl try:

Chinese Fried Quinoa with Spicy Garlic Sesame Oil
Vegetable Mains (p. 140)

Easy Chicken & Tomato Curry
Meat (p. 84)

Italian Chicken Stew
Meat (p. 81)

Keralan Turmeric Fish Curry
Fish (p. 120)

Mamma Mia Meatballs
Meat (p. 105)

Mushroom Bourguignon with Butternut Mash
Vegetable Mains (p. 156)

Pad Thai Noodles
Vegetable Mains (p. 136)

Spicy Nutty Noodles with Fried Eggs
Vegetable Mains (p. 138)

Thai Cauliflower Fried Rice with Prawns
Fish (p. 112)

Monday miso noodle soup

Soothing, easy and restorative, this is my ideal Monday night dinner. It will set you up nicely for the week. Although I always prefer a one-pan recipe, you do need two pans to keep things moving along. However, make it worthwhile by cooking extra noodles and eggs for the week ahead, so think of this recipe as both your Monday night dinner and an investment for the week ahead. You could add them to a Waste Not, Want Not Bowl (p. 72) for a packed lunch. Not to worry if you can't get seaweed, but do look out for it.

Serves 4

10g (about 8 tablespoons) seaweed, such as dulse or arame
330g buckwheat noodles
1 tablespoon coconut oil
3cm piece of ginger, finely chopped or grated
3 garlic cloves, finely chopped
1 fresh red chilli, deseeded and finely chopped (or to taste)
1 bunch of spring onions, sliced
200g shiitake mushrooms, roughly sliced
1.2 litres stock/bone broth (p. 278) or water
4 eggs, at room temperature
1 cabbage (400g), shredded

MISO STIR-IN
2 tablespoons miso paste (or to taste)
1 tablespoon hot water
Juice of ½ lemon

TO SERVE
Toasted sesame oil, for drizzling
1 tablespoon black sesame seeds
½ lemon, cut into 4 wedges
Sea salt

1. Soak the seaweed (if using) in water according to the packet instructions, then drain, rinse in fresh water and roughly chop before setting aside. Boil the kettle.

2. Fill a saucepan with boiling water and cook the noodles according to the packet instructions until al dente (about 5 minutes instead of the usual 6–8), then drain, rinse with cold water to stop them cooking, and set aside.

3. Meanwhile, melt the oil in a second, larger saucepan over a medium-high heat. Add the ginger, garlic, chilli and white parts of the spring onions and fry for 2 minutes, stirring occasionally.

4. Add the mushrooms and cook for 3–4 minutes, stirring occasionally, then add the stock and bring to the boil. Reduce to a medium simmer to cook for 2 minutes and then add the cooked noodles back to the pan to heat through for 1 minute before removing from the heat.

5. While the mushrooms are simmering, fill the original pan with boiling water and lower the eggs into the pan. Simmer over a medium heat for 6½ minutes (for a just-runny yolk), then cool the boiled eggs under cold water, peel and halve.

6. Remove the soup pan from the heat, drop in the shredded cabbage and the soaked seaweed, then mix together the 'miso stir-in' in a small bowl and stir through the soup.

7. Divide the soup among four bowls, add the egg halves and top with the remaining chopped spring onions and a drizzle of toasted sesame oil. Sprinkle the egg halves with sea salt and black sesame seeds and serve with a lemon wedge if you wish.

✳ Use It Up

Any cabbage will do here, or swap it for pak choi, broccoli or any leafy greens, and use any mushrooms you have.

Greek red lentil soup

This 20-minute soup is inspired by the Greek classic *fakes*. Red split lentils cook in less than 20 minutes and make for a speedy store cupboard dish. I love this topped with feta, which melts into the soup, and a mound of fresh herbs.

Serves 6

2 tablespoons butter or ghee
2 large onions, chopped
2 large carrots, chopped into
   2cm chunks
6 garlic cloves, finely chopped
2 handfuls of fresh parsley,
   stalks finely chopped and
   leaves roughly chopped
1 teaspoon dried oregano
   or thyme
1 teaspoon dried rosemary
2 bay leaves
500g red split lentils, rinsed
2 tablespoons tomato purée
1.8 litres stock/bone broth
   (p. 278) or water
300g spinach
2 tablespoon apple cider
   vinegar or red wine vinegar
Sea salt and black pepper

TO SERVE
Extra-virgin olive oil
200g feta, crumbled
1 lemon, cut into wedges

1. Melt the butter in a large saucepan, add the onions and fry on a medium heat for 4 minutes. Add the carrots, garlic, parsley stalks and dried herbs and cook for another 2 minutes, stirring occasionally.

2. Add the lentils with the tomato purée and the stock. Bring to a medium-high simmer, then cover with a lid and cook for 18 minutes until the lentils are tender and starting to fall apart. Stir halfway through and add some more water if you prefer the soup to be more liquid.

3. Stir in the spinach and vinegar, cook for a further minute and season with salt and pepper before dividing among six bowls.

4. Add a swirl of olive oil to each bowl, crumble over the feta and top with the parsley leaves. Serve with the lemon wedges.

✳ Use It Up

Replace the dried oregano and the dried rosemary with 1 tablespoon each of the chopped fresh herb. Parsley is used here but you could replace it with coriander, mint or dill (or a mixture if you have leftovers that need using up). Swap the spinach for any chopped leafy greens. Top with chunks of freshly fried halloumi (p. 35).

French lentil stew with gremolata

This simple and delicious dish is inspired by classic French stews. All the ingredients are easily found at your corner shop. Do make the gremolata, which you can put together in a few minutes. The gremolata is wonderful on fish, steak and roast vegetables, or you can use it as a dressing for a crispy salad. Any extra can be kept in the fridge for up to a week.

Serves 4

1 tablespoon butter or ghee
1 large onion, finely chopped
3 celery sticks, diced
3 carrots, diced
2 garlic cloves, finely chopped
1 teaspoon dried thyme or
  mixed herbs
1 x 400g tin of chopped
  tomatoes
400ml water or stock/bone
  broth (p. 278)
2 x 400g tins of lentils (Puy,
  brown or green), drained
  and rinsed
Sea salt and black pepper

GREMOLATA
1 tablespoon pine nuts
1 large handful of fresh
  parsley
Juice and grated zest of
  ½ lemon
4 tablespoons extra-virgin
  olive oil

TO SERVE
Extra-virgin olive oil
1 handful of grated Gruyère or
  mature Cheddar (optional)

1. Melt the butter in a large, wide pan, add the onion, celery and carrots and fry over a medium heat for 8 minutes until softened. Add the garlic and dried herbs and cook for a further minute.

2. Pour in the tinned tomatoes and water. Season with salt and pepper and bring to the boil, then reduce the heat to medium and simmer for 12 minutes.

3. Meanwhile, make the gremolata. Pulse everything together in a food processor or high-powered blender and taste for seasoning. Alternatively, chop up the pine nuts and parsley (cutting the stalks very finely) before mixing with the other ingredients.

4. Add the lentils to the soup and cook for a further 4 minutes, then taste for seasoning and remove from the heat.

5. Serve each bowl with a drizzle of the gremolata, or just swirl over some olive oil, if you prefer. Top with a little grated cheese.

✳ Use It Up

Swap the pine nuts for chopped Brazil nuts or other nuts or seeds.

Big-batch dahl with coriander yoghurt

This is not the traditional way to cook dahl, but it works just as well, especially if you're short on time. It's great just being able to add everything to one pot and leave it to do its work while you get on with other things. Aside from the yoghurt, citrus and fresh coriander, all of which you could leave out if you prefer, these are all store cupboard ingredients. Plenty of coconut gives it a creaminess and natural sweetness. Enjoy as it is or top with a fried or poached egg, and serve with naan (pictured), a quick slaw (p. 117) or vegetable rice (p. 272).

Serves 6

SPICES
1½ teaspoons ground
  turmeric
1 teaspoon ground cumin
2 teaspoons ground coriander
1 teaspoon mustard seeds
1 teaspoon chilli flakes
  (or to taste)

DAHL
1 large onion, finely chopped
3cm piece of ginger, grated
  or finely chopped
500g red split lentils, rinsed
Stalks of 2 large handfuls of
  fresh coriander, chopped
1.5 litres stock/bone broth
  (p. 278) or water
1 x 400ml tin of coconut milk
300g spinach
Juice of 1 lime or ½ lemon
1 tablespoon tamari
Sea salt
Seeds or toasted chopped
  cashews, to serve (optional)

CORIANDER YOGHURT
Leaves of 2 large handfuls of
  fresh coriander, chopped
300g natural yoghurt
Grated zest of 1 lime or
  ½ lemon
A pinch of sea salt

1. Sprinkle the spices over the base of a large, wide pan and toast over a medium heat for 1 minute, keeping an eye on them to make sure they don't burn.

2. Add the onions, ginger, lentils and coriander stalks, followed by the stock and coconut milk, and stir well. Bring to a medium simmer, cover with a lid and leave to cook for 18–20 minutes, stirring halfway through. You might want to add an extra 200ml of water during the cooking, depending on whether you like your dahl thicker or soupier in consistency.

3. Meanwhile make the coriander yoghurt by simply stirring everything together in a bowl, and season.

4. Stir in the spinach to heat through for 1 minute, with the lid on the pan.

5. Remove the dahl from the heat, add the lime juice, tamari and a little salt, give everything a stir and check for seasoning. Ladle into bowls, top with a heaped tablespoon of coriander yoghurt and a sprinkling of seeds or nuts (if using).

Lentil & bean chilli with guacamole

This warming chilli is delicious topped with a mound of guacamole. You could stretch this recipe to serve six people by serving with some Coriander & Lime Quinoa (p. 192) or cauliflower rice (p. 272). Swap the kidney beans for black beans, or indeed any type of beans, and amp up the cayenne pepper if you like.

Serves 4

1 tablespoon ghee
2 onions, finely chopped
2 garlic cloves, finely chopped
1 teaspoon dried oregano
   or thyme
1 large red pepper, deseeded
   and diced
2 carrots, diced
2 x 400g tins of chopped
   tomatoes
250ml stock/bone broth
   (p. 278) or water
2 handfuls of fresh
   coriander, stalks and leaves
   finely chopped
2 x 400g tins of kidney beans,
   drained and rinsed
2 x 400g tins of lentils
   (Puy, brown or green),
   drained and rinsed
Juice and grated zest of 1 lime

SPICES
2 teaspoons ground cumin
2 teaspoons ground coriander
1 teaspoon smoked paprika
½ teaspoon cayenne pepper

GUACAMOLE
1 large avocado
Juice of 1 lime
4 spring onions, sliced
1 garlic clove, finely chopped
Sea salt and black pepper

TO SERVE (OPTIONAL)
1 handful of grated Cheddar
A dollop of soured cream
   or natural yoghurt

1. Melt the ghee in a wide, deep pan, add the onions and fry on a medium heat for 4 minutes. Add the garlic, dried herbs and spices and fry for a further minute.

2. Add the red pepper and carrots and cook for 5 minutes, stirring occasionally and adding a splash of water if it starts to stick.

3. Add the tinned tomatoes, stock and the coriander stalks. Bring to the boil, then reduce the heat to medium and simmer for 15 minutes, uncovered, until reduced and thickened.

4. Meanwhile, prepare the guacamole by scooping out the avocado flesh into a bowl, roughly mashing and then stirring in the other ingredients, seasoning with salt and pepper to taste.

5. Turn up the heat, add the kidney beans and lentils to the pan and cook for a final 4 minutes and season to taste. Remove from the heat and divide between serving bowls. Add the lime juice, season to taste and top each bowl with a generous spoonful of guacamole and chopped coriander leaves. Serve with the grated cheese and some soured cream or yoghurt sprinkled with the lime zest.

Chunky tagine-style stew

A hearty stew inspired by a tagine, though simmered in a pan rather than a tagine pot (because I don't have one!). For ease, a good-quality harissa paste or powder, or a Moroccan spice mix like *ras el hanout,* would work perfectly here, though all the spices listed below are worth stocking up on, in any case. The vibrant green herbs give a lovely touch of freshness, and if you have any olives, dried fruit such as raisins or apricots, chopped preserved lemon, or chopped toasted nuts, then add those in too.

Serves 4

1 tablespoon coconut oil
  or ghee
2 onions, roughly chopped
3 garlic cloves, finely chopped
3cm piece of ginger, finely
  chopped
2 large carrots, cut into
  1.5cm chunks
1 aubergine, chopped into
  2cm cubes
2 large courgettes, chopped
  into 2cm cubes
1 x 400g tin of chopped
  tomatoes
2 large handfuls of fresh
  coriander, stalks finely
  chopped and leaves
  roughly chopped
200ml stock/bone broth
  (p. 278) or water
2 x 400g tins of aduki beans,
  drained and rinsed
1 tablespoon maple syrup
Juice and grated zest of
  ¼ lemon
Sea salt and black pepper

SPICES
1 teaspoon ground cinnamon
2 teaspoons ground cumin
2 teaspoons smoked paprika
1 teaspoon chilli flakes
  (or to taste)

1. Melt the oil in a large, wide pan, add the onions and fry over a medium-high heat for 4 minutes to soften.

2. Add the garlic, ginger and spices to the pan and stir-fry for a further 1 minute. Stir in the carrots and aubergine and cook for another 3 minutes, adding a splash of water if the mixture is looking dry.

3. Add the courgettes, tomatoes, coriander stalks and stock and stir to combine. Bring to the boil, then reduce to a medium simmer to cook for 12 minutes, covered, until the vegetables are just tender. If using preserved lemon, olives or dried fruit, add now.

4. Add the aduki beans, season with salt and pepper and simmer for another 4 minutes, with the lid off the pan, to thicken.

5. Remove from the heat, add the maple syrup, along with the lemon juice, taste for seasoning and serve scattered with the coriander leaves and chopped nuts.

✳ Use It Up

Swap the aduki beans for other beans or lentils. Swap the fresh coriander for parsley or mint, or use a mixture of all three if you've got some of each and they need using up.

Lime & avocado gazpacho

A soup for summer! Make sure the avocado and tomatoes are ripe for this gazpacho, so that it's naturally full of flavour. The soup is best served chilled and silky smooth with a drizzle of extra-virgin olive oil. You could also add a touch of spices – smoked paprika and cumin. If you wanted to make it look a bit fancier, dice up some extra tomato, red pepper and cucumber, or snip up a handful of chives, and use to garnish.

Serves 6, as a starter

6 large tomatoes, halved and
    deseeded
1 small red pepper, halved
    and deseeded
1 large cucumber, halved
    lengthways and deseeded
1 small red onion, roughly
    chopped
1 large garlic clove, peeled
Flesh of 1 avocado
Juice of 1 lime
2 tablespoons extra-virgin
    olive oil, plus extra to serve
Sea salt and black pepper
Pinch of chilli flakes, to serve

1. Blend all the ingredients together in a food processor or high-powered blender, seasoning with salt and pepper to taste. Add some cold water if the mixture seems particularly thick; it should be a thin, creamy soup, bearing in mind that it will thicken more as it chills.

2. Chill in the fridge for 20 minutes, then serve with an extra drizzle of olive oil and a sprinkling of salt, pepper and chilli flakes.

Creamy watercress, pea & mint soup

Watercress is one of my favourite greens – delicious raw in salads or lightly cooked in soups and stews. Its pepperiness balances the sweetness of the peas in this really quick green soup. If you can't get watercress, substitute with spinach, which you could keep in the freezer with the peas, to make this a great store cupboard and freezer standby. The cooked white beans (or any beans of your choice) add extra creaminess and make this soup really satisfying. If you like, you could add a swirl of Tahini Lemon Drizzle (p. 146) or Garlic Yoghurt (p. 188). I love this soup with toasted Quick Quinoa Bread (p. 21) and butter.

Serves 4

1½ tablespoons butter or ghee
1 onion, roughly chopped
2 garlic cloves, roughly chopped
1 x 400g tin of white beans, drained and rinsed
600ml stock/bone broth (p. 278) or water
300g frozen peas
400g watercress (leaves and stalks), plus extra to serve
1 large handful of fresh mint leaves (see tip), plus extra to serve
1½ tablespoons lemon juice
Sea salt and black pepper
Extra-virgin olive oil, to serve

1. Melt the butter in a wide saucepan, add the onion and fry over a medium heat for 6 minutes to soften. Add the garlic to cook for the last 30 seconds.

2. Add the beans and stock. Bring to a simmer over a medium-high heat and cook for 2 minutes. Add the frozen peas to cook for another minute.

3. Drop in the watercress and mint leaves, stir and remove from the heat – the green leaves will wilt in the hot liquid.

4. Add the lemon juice and some salt and pepper, then transfer to a blender, or use a hand-held blender, and whizz into a smooth, creamy soup. Taste for seasoning and serve with a drizzle of olive oil and some extra mint and watercress leaves.

✳ Use It Up

For zero waste, save the mint stalks for making a pot of mint tea. If you have a little leftover rocket or lettuce languishing in the fridge, add it along with the watercress.

Ginger miso sunshine soup

A bright orange vegetable soup spiked with ginger, turmeric, miso and lemon juice that is also freezer friendly. This soup came about because I had some carrots and half a squash to hand, but feel free to use one or the other. It can be served either chunky or blended smooth. If you're not blending, chop up the vegetables more finely; if blending, just roughly chop, which will also save a little time. Be sure to make the chive topping, which is also delicious on grilled fish, chicken and roasted veg.

Serves 6

1 tablespoon coconut oil
 or ghee
2 large onions, roughly
 chopped
4 garlic cloves, roughly
 chopped
5cm piece of ginger, chopped
1 teaspoon ground turmeric
4 large carrots, chopped into
 1.5cm cubes
1 medium butternut squash,
 peeled, deseeded and
 chopped into 2cm cubes
1.5 litres stock/bone broth
 (p. 278) or water
2 tablespoons miso (or to taste)
Juice of 1 lemon
Sea salt and black pepper

CHIVE TOPPING
1 fresh red chilli, deseeded and
 finely chopped
4 tablespoons chives, chopped
4 tablespoons sunflower seeds
4 tablespoons extra-virgin
 olive oil
A pinch of sea salt

1. Melt the oil in a large, wide saucepan, add the onions and cook over a medium heat for 4 minutes, stirring from time to time. Add the garlic, ginger and turmeric and cook for a further minute.

2. Add the carrots and squash, followed by the stock. Bring to a medium simmer, cover with a lid and cook for 15–18 minutes until the vegetables are tender.

3. Meanwhile, mix together all the ingredients for the topping in a small bowl. Add the miso and lemon juice to another bowl with a few tablespoons of the hot liquid from the pan and stir or whisk into a smooth paste.

4. Remove the soup from the heat and stir through the miso paste. Use a blender, or hand-held blender, to blend the soup in batches (or leave chunky, if you prefer) and taste for seasoning – you can always add a little more miso/salt and pepper/lemon juice if you think it needs it – then serve with the chive topping.

••●• Time Saver

While the onion is frying, use the time to start prepping the squash.

Tuscan bean soup with Parmesan bites

This is a great soup for when you feel you're lacking in greens and want something both quick and nourishing. Any greens or beans will go here and any herbs and spices too – this is one of the best recipes to have up your sleeve so play around with it. If you want to double up the recipe and eat the rest later or freeze it, then don't add cabbage to the portion you're saving but stir it through when you reheat the soup. If you don't fancy making the Parmesan bites, then just grate a little Parmesan or pecorino over the top when serving and let it melt in.

Serves 4

1 tablespoon butter or ghee
1 large onion, diced
1 fennel bulb, diced (fronds saved to garnish)
3 garlic cloves, finely chopped
1½ teaspoons rosemary, thyme or dried mixed herbs
½ teaspoon chilli flakes (or to taste – optional)
1 small cabbage, such as Savoy, (about 300g), shredded
2 x 400g tins of beans (such as borlotti or cannellini), drained and rinsed
700ml stock/bone broth (p. 278) or water
1 teaspoon apple cider vinegar
Sea salt and black pepper

TO SERVE
Extra-virgin olive oil
50g Parmesan or pecorino, grated

1. Melt the butter in a large, wide saucepan, add the onion and fennel and fry over a medium heat for 6 minutes, to soften. Add the garlic, herbs and chilli (if using) and cook for another minute.

2. Place the cabbage in the pan, then season and cook for another 2 minutes with a splash of water, stirring occasionally.

3. Add the beans (see tip), along with the stock. Bring to the boil, then reduce to a medium simmer and cook, with a lid on, for 2 minutes until the cabbage is tender. Season to taste, but remember that the Parmesan is quite salty.

4. Divide the soup among bowls, drizzling a swirl of olive oil on top. Immediately wipe out the soup pan with kitchen paper so that it's dry, turn up the heat and make four circles of grated Parmesan (each about 4cm diameter) in the pan. Allow the cheese to crisp up for 1 minute, then flip over and fry on the other side for about 30 seconds until golden.

5. Serve each Parmesan bite on top of a bowl of soup and garnish with the fennel fronds.

✳ Use It Up

Replace the cabbage with other leafy greens, such as cavolo nero or kale. If using kale, pull the leaves off the thick stems and roughly chop, discarding the stems, then cook for an extra minute.

● Tip

For a thicker soup, use a fork or potato masher to roughly mash up about a quarter of the beans before adding them to the pan.

Family-favourite sausage stew

A very comforting stew with celeriac chunks – a great alternative to potato in stews and mash (p. 274) – and lots of leafy greens. Look for good-quality sausages made without breadcrumbs added to bulk them out. I've made this before with lamb merguez sausage meat, which was especially delicious because of the fiery spices. Look out for the Swiss and beautiful rainbow varieties of chard. Don't throw away the stalks – just chop them finely.

Serves 4

1 tablespoon butter or ghee
1 large onion, chopped
1 teaspoon dried rosemary or
   mixed herbs
½ teaspoon fennel seeds
½ teaspoon chilli flakes
   (or to taste)
3 garlic cloves, finely chopped
6 sausages (about 400g)
3 tablespoons tomato purée
1 tablespoon apple cider
   vinegar
600ml stock/bone broth
   (p. 278) or water
1 celeriac (800g), peeled and
   chopped into 1.5cm cubes
1 handful of fresh parsley,
   stalks finely chopped and
   leaves roughly chopped
300g chard
Sea salt and black pepper
Extra-virgin olive oil, to serve

1. Melt the butter in a large wide pan, add the onion, herbs, fennel seeds and chilli flakes and fry over a medium heat for 4 minutes until softened, stirring occasionally. Add the garlic and cook for another minute.

2. Meanwhile, slice down the length of the sausage casings and remove the sausage meat. Discard the casing and add the meat to the pan and let it brown for about 4 minutes, stirring occasionally and breaking it up with a wooden spoon.

3. Turn up the heat, add the tomato purée and the vinegar and let the mixture bubble away for 30 seconds while stirring with the wooden spoon to scrape up any bits stuck to the bottom of the pan.

4. Pour in the stock, add the celeriac, parsley stalks and a pinch of salt and pepper and bring to a medium simmer. Cover with a lid and cook for 18–20 minutes until the celeriac is just tender.

5. Meanwhile, prepare the chard. Cut the stalks from the leaves, then finely chop the stalks and slice the leaves into ribbons 1cm wide. Add the chopped chard to the stew to cook for 2–3 minutes, then taste for seasoning and serve up each bowl with a drizzle of olive oil and with the chopped parsley leaves scattered over.

✳ Use It Up

Replace the sausages with 400g of pork or lamb mince, and swap the chard for another leafy green vegetable, such as kale or spring greens. Use a combination of celeriac and carrots if you like (total 800g).

Spanish chickpea & almond stew

Using store cupboard staples and spinach from the freezer, this Seville-inspired stew comes together in under 20 minutes and is a hit with everyone. You could swap the spinach for other greens, such as chopped chard, or add extra bits and bobs, such as a few tablespoons of capers, olives or chopped sun-dried tomatoes. I love this as a stew-like soup in a bowl, but you could make it thicker and serve with a side of quinoa (p. 150).

Serves 4

3 tablespoons chopped or
   flaked almonds
1½ tablespoons butter or ghee
1 large onion, finely chopped
1 large red or orange pepper,
   deseeded and chopped
3 garlic cloves, finely chopped
1 large handful of fresh
   parsley, stalks finely chopped
   and leaves roughly chopped
1 tablespoon tomato purée
2 x 400g tins of chopped
   tomatoes
2 x 400g tins of chickpeas,
   drained and rinsed
100ml stock/bone broth
   (p. 278) or water (optional)
250g spinach
1 tablespoon lemon juice
Sea salt and black pepper
Extra-virgin olive oil, to serve

SPICES
2 teaspoons ground cumin
2 teaspoons smoked paprika
¼ teaspoon cayenne pepper

1. In a large, deep frying pan, toast the almonds over a medium heat for just under a minute until golden, then set aside. Melt the butter in the hot pan, add the onion and pepper and fry for 6 minutes until starting to soften.

2. Add the garlic, spices and parsley stalks and fry for 1 minute, stirring constantly to prevent them from burning, then add the tomato purée and cook for another 30 seconds.

3. Tip the tinned tomatoes into the pan, turn up the heat to a medium simmer and cook for 15 minutes, uncovered, to thicken and reduce. Add the chickpeas and cook for another 3 minutes with a lid on. If you want the stew to be more soup-like, add the stock.

4. Turn up the heat, drop in the spinach and cook for 1 minute, covered with the lid, then add the lemon juice and season with salt and pepper.

5. Serve each bowl with a good drizzle of olive oil and with the parsley leaves and toasted almonds scattered over.

Easy ratatouille

Full of vibrant summer vegetables – aubergines, peppers, courgettes and tomatoes – this ratatouille has a hint of caponata courtesy of the olives, capers and basil, making it a bit of an Italian/French mash-up. It's delicious served either hot or cold, with a sprinkling of toasted pine nuts and dotted with ricotta, mozzarella or feta. Enjoy as a side or with some Basil & Lemon Quinoa (p. 192), as pictured here. Any leftovers can be reheated, uncovered, to reduce and thicken, or served as a pasta sauce or with fried eggs on top for brunch.

Serves 4 as a main or 6 as a side

2 tablespoons butter or ghee
1 large red onion, finely chopped
4 garlic cloves, finely chopped
2 teaspoons dried thyme
½ teaspoon chilli flakes
2 large handfuls of fresh basil, stalks finely chopped and leaves roughly torn
1 large aubergine, cut into 1.5cm cubes
2 large courgettes, halved and cut into 1.5cm slices
1 large red pepper, deseeded and cut into 1.5cm cubes
3 tablespoons tomato purée
2 tablespoons capers
12 pitted olives, halved
300g cherry tomatoes or 3 tomatoes, chopped
500ml stock/bone broth (p. 278) or water
1 tin 400g chickpeas or beans, drained and rinsed
Sea salt and black pepper

TO SERVE
2 tablespoons pine nuts
Extra-virgin olive oil
100g creamy cheese (such as ricotta, feta or mozzarella)
1 handful of flat leaf parsley leaves, roughly torn

1. In a wide frying pan, dry-toast the pine nuts (to serve) on a medium heat for about a minute, tossing occasionally to make sure they don't burn, then set aside.

2. Melt the butter in the same pan, add the onion and fry over a medium heat for 4 minutes, stirring every now and then, until starting to soften.

3. Add the garlic, dried herbs, chilli and basil stalks and cook for 1 minute, then add the aubergine, courgette and red pepper and fry for 4 minutes, stirring occasionally. Scrape away any bits that start to stick and add a splash of water if the mixture starts looking dry.

4. Turn up the heat, stir through the tomato purée and cook for 30 seconds, then add the capers, olives, tomatoes and stock. Season to taste with salt and pepper and bring to a medium simmer. Cook for 18 minutes, uncovered, adding the beans for the last 5 minutes, until it's lovely and thick. Put a lid on the pan if you prefer it soupier and add more liquid if you like. Make the Basil & Lemon Quinoa while the ratatouille cooks.

5. Divide among bowls and drizzle each portion with olive oil. Top with the toasted pine nuts and/or cheese and serve with the torn basil leaves or some parsley leaves as well, if you like.

● Tip

Increase the liquid by another 200ml and add a (further) tin of beans or lentils to make a hearty one-pot stew, which you could top with pesto (p. 67) to serve.

Sweet potato & cauliflower curry

This gently spiced yellow curry gets its colour from the turmeric and creaminess from the coconut milk. I like to keep it chunky, but you could blend it into a smooth soup. You could also swap the sweet potatoes for carrots, squash, celeriac, swede or indeed any root vegetable. To make any leftovers go further, serve with some quick slaw or add a handful of cooked beans or lentils.

Serves 4

1 tablespoon coconut oil
  or ghee
1 large onion, diced
2 garlic cloves, finely chopped
3cm piece of ginger, grated
1 teaspoon ground turmeric
1 teaspoon ground coriander
1 handful of fresh coriander,
  stalks finely chopped and
  leaves kept whole
2 tablespoons tomato purée
4 sweet potatoes, chopped
  into 1.5cm cubes
1 x 400ml tin of coconut milk
300ml stock/bone broth
  (p. 278) or water
1 large cauliflower
  (about 900g), chopped into
  equal-sized florets
1 tablespoon tamari or a big
  pinch of sea salt
Juice of ½ lime

1. Melt the oil in a wide pan, add the onion and fry over a medium heat for 5 minutes until softened. Add the garlic, ginger, spices and coriander stalks and cook for a further minute before stirring in the tomato purée.

2. Add the sweet potato cubes, coconut milk and stock, then bring to a medium simmer and cook for 10 minutes with the lid on the pan.

3. Remove the lid, add the cauliflower and simmer for another 5 minutes until all the vegetables are tender, but not soft, and the sauce has thickened and is beginning to reduce.

4. Add the tamari or sea salt and the lime juice, taste for seasoning and scatter over the coriander leaves to garnish.

Courgette risotto with a pesto swirl

A quinoa risotto is super quick and easy as you don't need to watch the pot and stir it. The pesto can be made in advance and kept in the fridge to use in pesto chicken (p. 78) or to liven up soups or a Waste Not, Want Not Bowl (p. 72). Feel free to add more green vegetables to the risotto, if you like – a handful of fresh or frozen peas, baby broad beans or chopped asparagus stirred in at the end to heat through.

Serves 4

1½ tablespoons butter or ghee
1 large onion, finely chopped
3 garlic cloves, finely chopped
250g quinoa, well rinsed
   (ideally soaked first, p. 277)
1 small glass of white wine
   (175ml)
600ml stock/bone broth
   (p. 278) or water
4 large courgettes (total 700g),
   roughly grated
100g Parmesan, grated

PESTO
2 very large handfuls of fresh
   basil (leaves and stalks), plus
   extra leaves to garnish
1 garlic clove, peeled
1 small handful of pine nuts
4 tablespoons extra-virgin
   olive oil
Juice of ½ lemon
Sea salt and black pepper

1. Melt the butter in a wide pan on a medium heat, add the onion and cook for 5 minutes until softened. Add the garlic and fry for another minute, stirring occasionally.

2. Turn up the heat, add the quinoa and cook for a further minute to cook off any excess liquid and coat it in the onion and garlic mix.

3. Deglaze the pan with the wine and let it reduce for a minute. Then add 500ml of the stock and bring to a medium simmer to cook for 15 minutes until tender. (If the quinoa has been soaked first, add 400ml of liquid and cook for 12 minutes.)

4. Meanwhile, make the pesto. Finely chop the basil, garlic and pine nuts and stir in olive oil and lemon juice, adding salt and pepper to taste. Alternatively, pulse all the ingredients in the mini bowl attachment of a food processor.

5. About 10 minutes from the end of the cooking time, add the courgettes with a small pinch of salt (bearing in mind that Parmesan is salty) and a big pinch of pepper. Bring back up to a medium simmer and cook until the quinoa and courgettes are tender and the mixture has about the same amount of liquid as a standard risotto.

6. Take off the heat, stir in the grated Parmesan to melt and taste for seasoning. Top with a swirl of pesto to serve.

●●●● Time Saver

If you'd rather not make the pesto, just tear lots of basil leaves over at the end and add a drizzle of extra-virgin olive oil and a squeeze of lemon juice.

✳ Use It Up

Swap the wine for 2 tablespoons of lemon juice and an extra 150ml broth/stock or water. Swap the pine nuts in the pesto for cashews or Brazil nuts, and use pecorino instead of Parmesan.

Malaysian noodle soup

Two of my vegetarian friends made something similar for me about ten years ago when we were all in a Devon house together in the depths of winter and the boiler wasn't working properly. This warmed us up instantly and I remember thinking it was one of the most delicious things I had ever eaten. Double or triple the amount of spice paste you make and store in the freezer. It can be used to brighten up any soup or as the base for a fish or chicken curry. You could swap the noodles for chopped squash, or use cooked lentils, quinoa or beans.

Serves 4

330g buckwheat noodles
1 tablespoon extra-virgin
    olive oil
2 large carrots
1 x 400ml tin of coconut milk
200ml stock/bone broth
    (p. 278) or water
350g spinach
1 tablespoon fish sauce

SPICE PASTE
1 large red onion, roughly
    chopped
2 lemongrass stalks, tough
    outer leaves removed,
    roughly chopped
1 fresh red chilli, deseeded
    (or to taste)
3 garlic cloves, peeled
3cm piece of ginger, roughly
    chopped
Stalks from 1 large handful of
    fresh coriander (leaves saved
    to garnish)
2 tablespoons curry powder
Juice of 1 lime
1½ tablespoons coconut oil
A big pinch of sea salt

TO SERVE
2 tablespoons cashew nuts
1 lime, cut into 4 wedges
Chilli flakes

1. Scatter the cashew nuts (to serve) in a large, dry frying pan and toast over a medium heat for a minute or so, tossing occasionally to make sure they don't burn, then set aside.

2. In the same pan, cook the noodles according to the packet instructions until al dente (about 5 minutes instead of the usual 6–8). Rinse with cold water to stop them cooking further and toss in the olive oil to prevent them from sticking.

3. Meanwhile, blend all the spice paste ingredients together in a food processor or high-powered blender. Using the same pan as before, wiped clean with kitchen paper, fry the paste on a medium heat for about 5 minutes, stirring occasionally, until the raw ingredients no longer smell as pungent.

4. Meanwhile make carrot 'noodles' using a spiralizer or julienne/ standard vegetable peeler (p. 273).

5. Add the coconut milk and stock to the pan and stir well. Bring to a medium simmer to cook for 5 minutes, lid on, then stir in the spinach and the carrot noodles and cook for another minute.

6. Return the cooked buckwheat noodles to the pan, add the fish sauce and cook for 1 minute to warm through, then remove from the heat and taste for seasoning. Serve each bowl topped with the reserved coriander leaves, toasted nuts and lime wedges.

✳ Use It Up

Swap the carrots for two large courgettes. Replace the spinach with chard or kale and cook for 3 minutes in step 5.

Coconut mushroom & chicken soup

This delicious soup is inspired by the Thai classic *tom kha gai*, but I've replaced the traditional kaffir leaves with lime zest and juice, and the galangal with ginger, as they aren't so widely available – or not yet! If you can get them, keep them in the freezer, along with lemongrass. Swap the chicken with chunks of butternut squash, if you prefer, and try to use stock/bone broth here, rather than water, as it really makes a difference to the taste.

Serves 4 as a starter

2 chicken thighs (skin on and
   bone in; total 250g)
2 lemongrass stalks, tough
   outer leaves removed,
   finely sliced
3cm piece of ginger, finely
   chopped or grated
Juice and grated zest of
   ½–1 lime (or to taste)
1 large handful of fresh
   coriander, stalks finely
   chopped and leaves
   kept whole
250ml stock/bone broth
   (p. 278)
1 x 400ml tin of coconut milk
400g shiitake or oyster
   mushrooms, sliced
1 teaspoon chilli flakes
   (or to taste)
1 tablespoon fish sauce
1 tablespoon tamari
Sea salt

1. Place the chicken thighs and sliced lemongrass in a medium saucepan with the ginger, lime zest and coriander stalks. Pour in the stock and bring to the boil, with a lid on the pan, then reduce to a medium simmer and poach the chicken for 20–22 minutes until it's cooked through. Remove the chicken and transfer to a shallow bowl to rest.

2. Using the same pan, add the coconut milk and mushrooms, half the chilli and the fish sauce. Bring to a medium simmer and cook for 6 minutes while you roughly shred the chicken with two forks.

3. Return the chicken to the pan and add the tamari, lime juice and a little salt to taste. Divide the soup among bowls and serve with the coriander leaves and the rest of the chilli scattered over.

✳ Use It Up

Substitute the chicken thighs for 120g cooked chicken or fish. Shred and add to the soup to heat through for 2–3 minutes before serving.

If you don't have shiitake or oyster mushrooms, any kind of mushrooms will do instead.

Waste not, want not bowl

Do you embrace leftovers? If so, here's some inspiration for a delicious and quick bowl that uses up bits and bobs in the fridge. It's a very satisfying, time-efficient and economical habit to get into, and means you'll never waste food again! The bowl comes together in less than 15 minutes and it makes a brilliant breakfast on-the-go or to enjoy at any time of day. I've given a few ideas below, but you can substitute with anything that might be languishing in your vegetable drawer. Bold is best for the dressing: use one of the dressings listed below, or you can whip up a simple dressing of extra-virgin olive oil and lemon juice, seasoned with a pinch of salt and pepper.

Serves 1

BASE (1 HANDFUL)
Cooked quinoa (p.150), lentils
  or beans (p. 271)
Roasted vegetables (such as
  squash, sweet potato or
  leftover Vegetable Tray
  Bake, p. 204)

PROTEIN (1 HANDFUL)
Smoked salmon, trout or
  mackerel, sliced or flaked
1 boiled egg, halved or
  quartered
Leftover Spiced Beans (p. 35)
Roasted chicken, shredded
Tinned sardines

VEGETABLES (2 HANDFULS)
Salad leaves (such as
  watercress, rocket, red
  cabbage or shredded lettuce)
Leftover cooked greens (such
  as spinach or shredded
  chard, kale or cabbage)
Other leftover cooked
  vegetables (such as sliced
  mushrooms or roasted
  cauliflower florets)
Leftover raw vegetables (such
  as cherry tomatoes,
  cucumber slices, grated
  carrot or sliced avocado)
Leftover slaw (p. 177)

1. Build your bowl in handfuls. First add your base (1 handful), then your choice of protein (1 handful), followed by your choice of vegetables (2 handfuls) and toss with one of the dressings.

2. Lastly, add a bit of crunch with one or more of the toppings, along with any of the flavour boosters, if you like.

My seasonal favourites

Winter bowl: Combine 1 handful of cooked shredded kale, 1 handful of watercress, 1 handful of roasted shredded chicken and 1 handful of roast butternut squash chunks. Toss with leftover Tahini Lemon Drizzle (p. 146) and sprinkle with chopped dried cranberries.

Summer bowl: Combine 1 handful of cooked quinoa, 1 quartered hard-boiled egg, 1 handful of rocket and 1 handful of halved cherry tomatoes. Toss in leftover pesto (p. 67) as the dressing. Top with 1 tablespoon of sauerkraut and sprinkle with chilli flakes.

DRESSING OPTIONS

Pesto (p. 67)

Ginger Tahini Dressing
  (p. 166)

Garlic Yoghurt Dressing
  (p. 183)

Tahini Lemon Drizzle (p. 146)

Lemon Herb Drizzle (p. 87)

TOPPING OPTIONS

1 tablespoon chopped nuts
  or seeds

1 tablespoon dried fruit

1 tablespoon sauerkraut,
  kimchi or Quickly Pickled
  Veg (p. 199)

FLAVOUR BOOSTERS

Leftover fresh herbs (such as
  basil, parsley, mint or
  chives), chopped

Crumbled feta or goat's cheese
  or grilled halloumi slices
  (p. 35)

Spice mix (harissa, za'atar or
  chilli flakes)

MEAT

'AMONG the dishes in this chapter, you'll find new takes on some of the most beloved takeaways – I call them 'fakeaways'! They are quick to make, faster than waiting for a home delivery, packed full of flavour and, what's more, they really hit the spot. Take a look at the Hoisin Duck Pancakes (p. 92), Chicken Katsu Curry (p. 85), Parmesan Chicken Goujons (p. 80) or the Beef & Carrot Koftas (p. 94).'

While the focus is on meat here, there are plenty of vegetables too. The amount of meat may be slightly less than what you're used to, but with the combination of flavours and textures and the other nutrient-rich components of the meal, you'll find each dish substantial and satisfying overall. Don't worry: you won't feel you're missing out, and you certainly won't be going hungry!

You can easily make meat go further in dishes such as curries and stews by chopping up vegetables to simmer away with the meat, or make easy and satisfying side dishes, such as a cauliflower rice, celeriac mash or courgette noodles (pp. 272-274). For meatballs and koftas, grated carrot is added to the mix, helping to bulk out the meat, as well as adding extra juiciness and sweetness.

Meat is an expensive ingredient, but it's important to buy the best-quality meat you can afford; if you haven't got a good local butcher, have a look online. There are British farms who will post you a box of meat at a good price that you can keep in the freezer to use when you need it. (See also the Cooking Notes on p. 10 about buying organic produce, and the note on p. 265 about safely defrosting meat.)

One way to enjoy meat is to use cheaper cuts. Check out the onglet cut of beef in the Spicy Thai Beef Salad (p. 182), which is a fraction of the price of sirloin, whilst chicken thighs and drumsticks are always cheaper and juicier than breasts. Any type of mince can be used in the Spiced Lamb (p. 97) or Asian Turkey and Carrot Burgers (p. 90), for instance, and if you don't eat pork, you can use any kind of sausages in the Sausage & Kale Tray Bake (p. 100).

As this book is all about fast, 30-minute meals, it's not possible to slow-cook within this time frame, but by adding certain ingredients – such as the anchovies and wine in the Italian Chicken Stew (p. 81) – you can give the sort of depth of flavour that comes from slow-cooking. Bear in mind that smaller pieces of meat cook more quickly. Go for smaller chicken pieces rather than very large ones, and chop up a chicken leg into a thigh and drumstick (or ask your butcher) to speed up the cooking. And when you do get time, try some cuts like oxtail or shin and slow-cook them. It will only take you 5 minutes to prep a slow-cooked meal, and then you just let the slow cooker or a big pot, lid on, on a low heat, do all the work.

For more ways to enjoy meat try:

BLT Salad with Asparagus
  Salads (p. 180)

Coconut Mushroom & Chicken Soup
  Bowl Food (p. 71)

Mug of Miso Egg Broth
  Snacks (p. 219)

Scotch Eggs
  Snacks (p. 222)

Family Favourite Sausage Stew
  Bowl Food (p. 61)

Spicy Thai Beef Salad
  Salads (p. 182)

Adapting for vegetarians and pescatarians

Any of these dishes can easily be adapted for vegetarians. The chicken in the katsu curry (p. 85) can be replaced by roast aubergine; the sausages in the tray bake (p. 100) could be swapped with cubes of butternut squash; and the Italian stew (p. 81) would work just as well with lentils and beans replacing the chicken. For pescatarians, swap in fish or seafood in the Easy Chicken & Tomato Curry (p. 84), Goujons (p. 80) or Pesto Chicken (p. 78).

One-pan pesto chicken with summer vegetables

I find pesto chicken so comforting, whether served hot, as it is here, or eaten cold as a salad. You could easily swap in alternative veg – in colder months, chopped kale, mushrooms or some sun-dried tomatoes would be perfect. Serve this on its own or with cauliflower mash or rice (p. 274 and 272). Anything leftover would make a great packed lunch. Homemade pesto is very easy but look out for good-quality pesto in extra-virgin olive oil in the shops.

Serves 4

1½ tablespoons ghee
4 chicken breasts or thighs
  (boneless; total 500g),
  sliced into 2cm chunks
1 quantity of pesto (p. 67)
1 teaspoon chilli flakes, plus
  extra to serve (optional)
2 large courgettes, halved
  lengthways and sliced
350g asparagus spears, woody
  ends snapped off
300g cherry tomatoes, halved
Sea salt and black pepper

TO SERVE
200g rocket or watercress
Extra-virgin olive oil
1 lemon, cut into 4 wedges
1 handful of Parmesan
  shavings (optional)

1. Melt 1 tablespoon of ghee in a large, wide frying pan, add the chicken and fry over a high heat for 3 minutes. Using tongs or two forks, turn the pieces over and cook on the other side for another 3 minutes until golden all over and just cooked through. Meanwhile, make the pesto.

2. Transfer the chicken pieces to a bowl with the pesto, stirring to coat the chicken, and set aside.

3. Place the pan back over a high heat, melt the remaining ghee and add the chilli flakes (if using) and courgettes and fry for 1 minute, then tip in the asparagus and cook for another 2 minutes. Stir in the tomatoes, season with salt and pepper, and fry for a final minute until the green vegetables are tender and the tomatoes are just softened but still hold their shape.

4. Meanwhile, divide the rocket or watercress among individual plates, or make a bed of leaves on a serving platter, and drizzle with olive oil.

5. Return the pan to the hob and add the pesto-coated chicken to warm through on a low heat for a minute.

6. Divide the cooked vegetables among the plates, pile the chicken on top and serve with extra chilli flakes (if using), lemon wedges and some Parmesan scattered over the salad leaves, if you like.

✳ Use It Up

If asparagus isn't in season, replace with trimmed green beans or small broccoli florets. They need a bit longer to cook, so add to the pan first and cook for 1 minute before adding the courgettes. If you make your own pesto, add other leftover herbs along with the basil.

Parmesan chicken goujons with an avocado ranch dip

These quick-cooking goujons are irresistible for both grown-ups and kids alike. They would go well with squash fries (p. 206) – made without the Parmesan coating as there is already cheese in the goujons – and this creamy avocado dip or the Spiced Ketchup (p. 206). Any leftover goujons would be great in a wrap (p. 190) with shredded cabbage and a squeeze of lemon. Slice the goujons up into thin strips or nugget shapes if you prefer, just keep them an equal size for even cooking. Make double or triple quantities so you can have them ready to go from the freezer during a busy week.

Serves 4

1½ tablespoons ghee
140g ground almonds
40g Parmesan, grated
2 eggs
4 chicken breasts (skinless and boneless; total 500g), sliced
Sea salt and black pepper

OPTIONAL EXTRAS
1 teaspoon dried oregano or rosemary
½ teaspoon garlic or onion powder

AVOCADO RANCH DIP
Flesh of 1 large avocado
1-2 tinned anchovy fillets or 2 teaspoons Worcestershire sauce
1 large garlic clove, finely chopped or grated
1 teaspoon mustard
2 teaspoons maple syrup
1 tablespoon water
1½ tablespoons apple cider vinegar

1. Preheat the oven to fan 220°C/Gas mark 6. Add the ghee to a baking tray and place in the oven for a few minutes for the ghee to melt. Tip the tray so the melted ghee covers it and then pour into a small jug.

2. Pour the ground almonds and grated Parmesan into a bowl, add 1 teaspoon of salt and ½ teaspoon of pepper, plus any optional extras, and mix together. Crack the eggs into a second bowl and beat with a fork.

3. Dip the chicken slices first into the beaten eggs, then into the mixed almonds and Parmesan, making sure that each slice is fully coated in the mixture. Place on the greased baking tray and pour over the melted ghee.

4. Bake in the oven for 15–18 minutes, turning the goujons over halfway through, until cooked through and golden brown. Test one goujon by piercing with a sharp knife to see that the juices run clear.

5. Meanwhile, whizz all the dip ingredients together in a blender or food processor, seasoning with salt and pepper to taste.

6. Remove the goujons from the oven and serve with the dip and your choice of accompaniments.

✳ Use It Up

Swap the Parmesan for pecorino, if you prefer, or substitute with 40g desiccated coconut or extra ground almonds.

Italian chicken stew

An easy and hearty stew made with olives, herbs and mushrooms. Be sure to use a wide, deep pan with a lid for this as it really reduces the cooking time. The anchovy fillets and wine give a good depth of flavour that normally comes from long, slow cooking. You could replace the anchovies with a tablespoon of capers or a handful of sun-dried tomatoes, if you preferred. Serve with cauliflower or celeriac mash (p. 274) or a big green salad.

Serves 4

2 tablespoons ghee
1 large onion, roughly
  chopped
2 teaspoons dried mixed herbs
400g mushrooms (such as
  portobello), roughly chopped
2 carrots, sliced
4 garlic cloves, finely chopped
3 tinned anchovy fillets
1 large handful of fresh
  parsley, stalks finely chopped
  and leaves roughly chopped
4 chicken thighs (skin on and
  bone in; total 600g)
1 handful of pitted green
  olives
1 small glass of red wine
  (175ml)
1 x 400g tin of chopped
  tomatoes
200ml stock/bone broth
  (p. 278) or water
200g spinach
Sea salt and black pepper

1. Melt 1 tablespoon of the ghee in a large, wide pan, add the onion and dried herbs and fry over a medium-high heat heat for 5 minutes, stirring occasionally. Add the mushrooms, carrots, garlic, anchovies and parsley stalks and fry for another 2 minutes, then transfer to a bowl.

2. Add the rest of the ghee and, once it has melted, place the chicken pieces in a single layer, skin side down, in the hot pan. Turn the heat right up and fry for about 90 seconds, then turn the pieces over and cook for another minute so that they are browned on both sides.

3. Return the cooked vegetables in the bowl to the pan, along with all the other ingredients except the spinach, then season and give it a good stir. Bring to a medium simmer and cook, covered with a lid, for 20 minutes or until the chicken is cooked through and the juices run clear when pierced with a sharp knife. If watery, remove the lid and simmer for 2-3 minutes to reduce.

4. Add the spinach to cook for the final minute and taste for seasoning. Sprinkle over the chopped parsley leaves to serve.

● Tip

The wine can be replaced with 175ml stock or water and 1 tablespoon of apple cider vinegar.

Fajita party

I'm a big fan of drumsticks and thighs on the bone, but for a fast weeknight dish like this, strips of chicken breast or thigh meat work perfectly. A fajita spread is a great option for when you've got a group of people with different chilli preferences. Just put all the accompaniments on the table and let everyone help themselves; it also saves you time! A quick Salsa Salad (p. 176) or some Guacamole (p. 53) would also go down brilliantly.

Serves 4

2 tablespoons coconut oil
  or ghee
1 large red onion, sliced
2 garlic cloves, finely chopped
2 large peppers, deseeded and
  sliced into strips
1 large courgette, sliced into
  strips
4 chicken breasts or thighs
  (skinless and boneless; about
  500g), sliced into strips

FAJITA SPICES
2 teaspoons smoked paprika
2 teaspoons ground cumin
¼ teaspoon cayenne pepper
  (to taste) or chilli flakes
1½ teaspoons dried oregano
  or thyme
½ teaspoon sea salt

TO SERVE
8 large lettuce or red cabbage
  leaves
1–2 fresh chillies, deseeded
  and finely chopped (to taste)
2 limes, cut into wedges
100g soured cream (optional)
2 handfuls of grated mature
  Cheddar (optional)
Guacamole (p. 53)

1. Melt half the oil in a large, wide frying pan, add the onion and garlic and fry on a medium heat for 4 minutes to soften.

2. Meanwhile, mix the fajita spices, herbs and salt in a small bowl and then add half the mix to the pan, along with the pepper and courgette strips, and fry for a further 5 minutes. Transfer all the cooked vegetables from the pan into a serving bowl and cover with a plate to keep warm.

3. Melt the remaining oil in the pan, add the chicken strips, spreading them out in a single layer, and fry over a high heat for 2–3 minutes until nicely golden. Sprinkle over the rest of the fajita spices, then turn the chicken strips over and fry for another 2 minutes until the chicken is cooked through.

4. Meanwhile, lay the lettuce or cabbage leaves on a large plate to form wraps and place on the table with the chillies, lime wedges, soured cream and grated cheese (if using).

5. Add the cooked vegetables back to the chicken pan to warm through briefly and serve the chicken mixture straight from the pan, allowing people to assemble the fajitas themselves from all the ingredients on the table.

✳ Use It Up

Swap half the chicken for sliced mushrooms. Use leftover Buckwheat Naans or Chickpea Wraps (p. 19 and p. 190), warmed through in a dry pan, instead of lettuce/cabbage leaves.

Easy chicken & tomato curry

Chicken thighs or drumsticks work best in this dish, for their flavour and because they are easier not to overcook, though you could reduce the cooking time by using roughly chopped chicken breasts and simmering for 12–15 minutes. If the chicken is already at room temperature, this will reduce the cooking time slightly, so take it out of the fridge an hour or so before cooking. To mop up all the delicious sauce, serve with Buckwheat Naans (p. 191), or Broccoli or Cauliflower Rice (p. 272). If you prefer a drier curry, you can always reduce the sauce down at the end. I always double up on this family favourite and freeze half, then stir through the spinach when reheating.

Serves 4

1½ tablespoons coconut oil
  or ghee
4 chicken thighs (skin on and
  bone in; total 600g)
1 large onion, grated or finely
  chopped
2 garlic cloves, grated or finely
  chopped
3cm piece of ginger, grated or
  finely chopped
1 x 400g tin of chopped
  tomatoes
1 large handful of fresh
  coriander, stalks finely
  chopped and leaves roughly
  chopped
200ml boiling water
200g spinach
Juice of ½ lemon
Sea salt and black pepper

SPICES
2 teaspoons ground coriander
1½ teaspoon ground cumin
1 teaspoon ground turmeric
Seeds from 3 cardamom pods,
  crushed or chopped
½ teaspoon chilli flakes
  (or to taste)

1. Melt the oil in a large, wide pan, add the chicken pieces and brown over a high heat for 1½ minutes on each side. If the chicken is in danger of sticking or burning, add a splash of water.

2. Add the onion, garlic, ginger and spices to the pan with a pinch of salt, mix together and fry on a medium heat for 4 minutes, stirring occasionally and making sure they don't burn.

3. Add the tomatoes, coriander stalks and boiling water, give everything a good stir and put a lid on the pan. Bring to a medium simmer and cook for 20 minutes, stirring halfway through, until the chicken is fully cooked. Check the chicken is cooked through, and the juices are running clear, by piercing one thigh/drumstick with a sharp knife at the thickest point.

4. In the last minute of cooking, add the spinach and lemon juice, replace the lid and let the spinach wilt. Season to taste with salt and pepper and garnish with the coriander leaves to serve.

Chicken katsu curry

This Japanese fast-food dish is a favourite takeaway of all my friends, so I learned how to adapt it for quick home cooking. The carrot both sweetens and thickens the gently spiced curry sauce, while the ground almonds and desiccated coconut give the succulent chicken pieces that 'breaded' taste and texture. Serve with Cauliflower Rice (p. 272) and some Quickly Pickled Veg (p. 199).

Serves 4

4 chicken breasts (total 500g)
4 tablespoons ground almonds
2 tablespoons desiccated
  coconut
1 egg, beaten
1 tablespoons coconut oil
  or ghee
Sea salt and black pepper

CURRY SAUCE
1 tablespoon coconut oil
  or ghee
1 onion, chopped
4 garlic cloves, finely chopped
1½ tablespoons curry powder
1 large carrot, sliced into
  thin rounds
1 tablespoon tomato purée
500ml chicken stock/bone
  broth (p. 278) or water
2 teaspoons maple syrup
1 tablespoon tamari

1. First make the curry sauce. Melt the oil in a wide saucepan, add the onion and fry over a medium heat for 4 minutes, stirring occasionally, then add the garlic and curry powder and cook for another minute.

2. Add the carrot, tomato purée and stock and bring to the boil. Reduce the heat and simmer, covered with a lid, for 8–10 minutes until the carrots are tender.

3. Meanwhile, place the chicken breasts between two layers of baking parchment and use a rolling pin to pound them into pieces about 1cm thick (or ask your butcher to do this).

4. Place the ground almonds and coconut in a shallow bowl. Add the egg to a second bowl and season with salt and pepper. Dip each chicken escalope first in the egg, coating both sides, and then in the almond and coconut mixture.

5. Once the carrots are tender, add the maple syrup and tamari and blend, either in a blender or in the pan using a hand-held blender. Taste for seasoning. Simmer the blended sauce, uncovered, in the pan on a low heat to allow it to thicken and reduce, then cover again with the lid and turn off the heat so the sauce stays hot.

6. Meanwhile, melt 1 teaspoon of oil in a large frying pan set over a high heat, add the chicken (you may need to cook it in batches) and fry for 5 minutes on each side until golden brown and cooked through. Repeat with a second batch, keeping the first batch warm in a low oven. Serve the chicken with the sauce drizzled over.

✳ Use It Up

Swap the desiccated coconut with more ground almonds or any ground nuts you have to hand. For a veggie version, swap the chicken with squash wedges or baked aubergine.

Za'atar chicken tray bake with lemon herb drizzle

Za'atar makes a good roast chicken even better. The incredible, flavour-packed green drizzle goes beautifully with so many things – any leftovers can be stored in the fridge and added to soups and stews or spooned over fish. Don't worry if you haven't got all the herbs; just use what you have to hand. You could swap the chicken here for big chunks of squash or aubergine halves, and sprinkle those with za'atar instead. Any leftover chicken can be shredded and added to a Waste Not, Want Not Bowl (p. 72). Serve with a green salad.

Serves 4

1 tablespoon coconut oil
   or ghee
8 chicken thighs (skin on and
   bone in; total 600g)
2 large fennel bulbs, roughly
   chopped
2 large red peppers, deseeded
   and roughly chopped
2 large courgettes, roughly
   chopped
4 tablespoons za'atar mix, plus
   extra to serve
Sea salt and black pepper

LEMON HERB DRIZZLE
1 large handful each of fresh
   coriander, parsley and dill
Juice and grated zest of
   1 lemon
1 teaspoon chilli flakes
   (to taste)
2 large garlic cloves, finely
   chopped
100ml extra-virgin olive oil
Sea salt and black pepper

1. Preheat the oven to fan 220°C/Gas mark 9. Add the oil to a wide, deep roasting tin or ovenproof dish and leave in the oven for a few minutes to melt.

2. Place the chicken and chopped vegetables in the tin and toss together in the melted oil. Spread the vegetables out in the tin as much as possible to form a single layer with the chicken arranged on top, or use two trays if you need to.

3. Sprinkle over the za'atar, season with salt and pepper and roast in the oven for about 25 minutes, tossing all the ingredients halfway through, until the chicken is cooked, the juices running clear when pierced with a sharp knife.

4. Meanwhile prepare the lemon herb drizzle. Finely chop the stalks of the herbs and roughly chop the leaves, then add to a bowl and mix with all the other ingredients, seasoning with salt and pepper to taste. Alternatively, blitz everything in a food processor or high-powered blender.

5. Remove the roasting tin from the oven, spoon two-thirds of the lemon herb drizzle over the vegetables and serve the chicken sprinkled with extra za'atar and with the remaining drizzle in a bowl for anyone to add more if they like.

✳ Use It Up

For the fresh herbs, anything goes – mint and basil would be delicious here too, and even that last bit of rocket or watercress is welcome here. Include the stalks of any herb except mint, saving those for making fresh mint tea!

Korean chicken with sesame sprinkle

Chicken thighs (or drumsticks) are perfect for this dish, but you could use wings, especially if you like eating with your fingers. The Korean-inspired sauce would go well with any meat or fish, as well as vegetable and noodle stir-fries. Look out for Korean chilli powder, if you can, and be sure to make the topping – you'll be sprinkling it on everything! Serve these with the Herb & Pak Choi Salad (p. 171) and Vegetable Rice (p. 272), the Sesame Carrot & Courgette Noodles (p. 164), or a simple green salad as pictured here.

Serves 4

4 chicken thighs (skin on and
    bone in; total 600g)
1 onion, finely chopped or
    grated
4 garlic cloves, finely chopped
    or grated
3cm piece of ginger, finely
    chopped or grated
1 teaspoon chilli flakes or
    Korean chilli powder
    (or to taste)
1½ tablespoons toasted
    sesame oil
6 tablespoons tamari
2½ tablespoons apple cider
    vinegar
2 tablespoons maple syrup

SESAME SPRINKLE
4 tablespoons black and white
    sesame seeds
2 tablespoons fresh chives,
    chopped
2 tablespoons chopped fresh
    coriander
½ teaspoon chilli flakes or
    Korean chilli powder
    (or to taste)

1. Preheat the oven to fan 220°C/Gas mark 9.

2. Mix everything together (except the ingredients for the sesame sprinkle) in a large baking dish or roasting tin. Spread the chicken pieces out in a single layer, skin side down, and bake in the oven for 12 minutes.

3. Remove from the oven and toss everything in the dish. Turn the chicken skin side up and roast for another 12–15 minutes until golden and cooked through, the juices running clear when pierced with a sharp knife.

4. Meanwhile, prepare any sides, mix the sesame sprinkle ingredients together and sprinkle over the cooked chicken to serve.

✳ Use It Up

Make double then shred the chicken for a packed lunch salad that you'll be desperate to eat.

● Tip

The onion, garlic and ginger are grated for a more textured sauce, but you can blitz all the sauce ingredients together in a food processor if you prefer.

Asian turkey & carrot burgers in lettuce cups

These burgers will be a hit with the whole family. You could keep a portion of the mixture plain for kids and spice yours up with a bit of chilli, if you like. Any type of minced meat works well here and you can make them smaller too. I love bite-sized meatballs in a miso broth. The burgers are presented here in crunchy lettuce cups with sliced tomato and shredded red cabbage, but they would also go well with stir-fried greens or Vegetable Rice (p. 272).

Serves 4

BURGERS
500g minced turkey
2 carrots, grated
1 onion, grated
3cm piece of ginger, grated
3 garlic cloves, grated
1 egg
1 fresh chilli, deseeded
  and finely chopped,
  or chilli flakes
1 small handful of fresh
  coriander, finely chopped
1½ teaspoons Chinese
  five-spice powder
Sea salt and black pepper

TO SERVE
16 crunchy lettuce leaves
½ red cabbage, shredded
2 tomatoes, sliced
1 lime, cut into wedges

1. Preheat the oven to fan 220°C/Gas mark 9 and line a large baking tray or roasting tin with baking parchment.

2. Combine all the ingredients for the burgers in a large bowl, season with 1 teaspoon of salt and ¼ teaspoon of pepper and mix well. Using damp hands, divide the mixture and shape into four (or eight small) burgers. Place on the prepared tray and bake in the oven for 18–20 minutes, turning halfway through, until cooked through.

3. Place each cooked burger in two lettuce leaf cups, adding some shredded cabbage and sliced tomato, along with a squeeze of lime and a sprinkling of salt and pepper.

● Tip

You can barbecue or grill these too. Rub a little coconut oil or ghee onto the burgers and barbecue or grill them for 8 minutes on each side until cooked through.

Hoisin duck pancakes

While it would be impossible to recreate true Chinese-style duck at home, this version comes with a big thumbs-up from my family. It uses duck breasts, speedy to cook and widely available, and quick pancakes made with chickpea (or gram) flour. The best thing about the recipe is the hoisin sauce, brightened with orange juice or any citrus and creaminess from the tahini. It's simple to make and tastes like the real deal. It's such a versatile sauce too. Just a little will enhance the flavour of leftover vegetables and it's also brilliant with fish burgers (p. 114).

Serves 4

4 duck breasts (skin on; total 600g)
1 teaspoon Chinese five-spice powder
A good pinch of sea salt

HOISIN SAUCE
6 tablespoons tamari
3 tablespoons tahini or smooth nut/seed butter (p. 276)
1½ tablespoons maple syrup
3 tablespoons orange juice
2 garlic cloves, finely chopped
1½ teaspoons toasted sesame oil
1½ teaspoons Chinese five-spice powder

TO SERVE
12 small Chickpea Wraps (p. 190 – made plain, with no additions, and warmed through), or any wraps of your choice
Chilli flakes, to taste
1 cucumber, sliced into matchsticks
6 spring onions, sliced into matchsticks

1. Preheat the oven to fan 200°C/Gas mark 7.

2. With a sharp knife, score the fat of each duck breast in a criss-cross pattern, then sprinkle over half the five-spice powder and salt and rub in.

3. Make the hoisin sauce by whisking all the ingredients together in a bowl, then taste for seasoning and set aside.

4. Heat up a wide, ovenproof frying pan to a high heat (no oil needed) and place the duck breasts, skin side down, in the pan. Sprinkle over the rest of the spice and salt. Cook for 3 minutes or until most of the fat has rendered, and the duck skin is golden.

5. Turn the duck breasts over and cook for a further 30 seconds to seal the other side. Place the pan in the oven for the duck to finish cooking – 8 minutes for rare or 10 minutes for medium rare – then remove the duck and leave to rest on a chopping board for 10 minutes. Use this time to make the chickpea batter and, while the duck is resting, use the same pan to make the wraps.

6. Pour any excess duck fat from the pan into a bowl.

7. Cut the duck breasts into thin slices, sprinkle with chilli flakes and place on a serving plate with the hoisin sauce in a bowl. Put the chickpea wraps on another plate and place the sliced cucumber and spring onions in a separate bowl. Let everyone assemble their own pancakes, pouring or spooning the hoisin sauce over the duck before adding the other ingredients.

✳ Use It Up

Duck and orange go so well together, but if you don't have an orange, use 2 tablespoons of lemon juice in the hoisin sauce instead. Save the duck fat for frying vegetables.

Beef & carrot koftas with chopped salad

These minced beef koftas are a winner with the whole family. Carrot bulks out the kofta mix and adds juiciness, not to mention an extra portion of veg. The crunchy salad provides a refreshing contrast, enhanced by the yoghurt dressing. You could serve any leftover koftas in a wrap (p. 190) or make a really quick soup by simmering some greens in a pan of stock/broth and adding koftas to heat through at the end with a squeeze of lemon juice and some seasoning.

Serves 4

500g minced beef
2 large carrots, grated
1 onion, finely chopped
3 garlic cloves, finely chopped
1½ teaspoons ground cumin
1 teaspoon ground cinnamon
½ teaspoon chilli powder
1½ teaspoon dried thyme
1 egg
Sea salt and black pepper
1 quantity of Garlic Yoghurt
    Dressing (p. 183), to serve

CHOPPED SALAD
1 crunchy lettuce (such as cos),
    chopped
½ small red cabbage, chopped
1 cucumber, halved
    lengthways, deseeded
    and chopped
2 tomatoes, diced
Flesh of 1 avocado, cubed
1 handful of fresh parsley or
    mint leaves, finely chopped
Juice of ½ lemon
4 tablespoons extra-virgin
    olive oil
Sea salt and black pepper

1. Preheat the oven to fan 220°C/Gas mark 9, or the grill to high, and line a large baking tray with baking parchment.

2. Place the beef and carrots in a large bowl with the onion, garlic, spices, herbs and egg. Season with 1½ teaspoons of salt and 1 teaspoon of pepper and mix well.

3. Divide the mixture into 12 pieces and, using damp hands, shape each into a sausage-shaped kofta about 8cm long. Arrange on the lined baking tray and either bake in the oven for 10–12 minutes, or under the grill for 8 minutes, turning halfway through, until cooked and browned all over.

4. Meanwhile, place all the salad ingredients in a serving bowl and toss together, seasoning to taste with salt and pepper.

5. Serve the koftas with the salad and garlic yoghurt dressing. I like to drizzle some dressing over the salad and then have extra on the plate to dip the koftas in.

✳ Use It Up

Swap the beef with minced lamb, chicken or turkey, or use the same method with fish. Cooking times may vary, so make sure the koftas are cooked through.

Spiced lamb in baked aubergine boats

This quick spiced lamb could be presented in many different ways – in a Chickpea Wrap (p. 190), for instance, or to top a Buckwheat Pizza (p. 153) – but it is especially good on these baked aubergine boats. Look for long, thin aubergines and serve with a simple green salad. Add nuts or seeds to the mix; pistachio is my favourite here, as it adds a wonderful texture to the mince. Try drizzling with yoghurt or Garlic Yoghurt as pictured here.

Makes 8 small boats / Serves 4

4 aubergines
Sea salt and black pepper
1½ tablespoons coconut oil
  or ghee

SPICED LAMB
1 onion, finely chopped
500g minced lamb
2 garlic cloves, finely chopped
1 teaspoon ground cumin
½ teaspoon chilli flakes,
  ideally Aleppo pepper
  (pul biber)
2 tablespoons tomato purée
150ml hot water
1 small handful of pistachios,
  roughly chopped (optional)
Juice of ½ lemon
1 handful fresh mint leaves
Natural yoghurt or Garlic
Yoghurt (p. 183), for drizzling

1. Preheat the oven to fan 220°C/Gas mark 9. Add half the oil to two baking trays and pop in the oven for a few minutes to melt.

2. Meanwhile, slice the aubergines in half lengthways and score the flesh in a tight criss-cross pattern, slicing down to the skin, but taking care not to cut through it.

3. Remove the trays from the oven and brush each aubergine piece, skin side up, with the hot oil. Turn the aubergines over so they are skin side down and divide between then trays. Sprinkle with salt and bake for 20-25 minutes until the flesh is just soft.

4. While they're baking, start to prepare the lamb. Melt the remaining oil in a wide pan over a medium heat and gently fry the onions for 5 minutes until softened but not browned.

5. Add the minced lamb and fry on a high heat for 5 minutes until browned, then add the garlic, cumin, chilli and tomato purée and cook for a further couple of minutes.

6. Pour in the hot water, bring to a medium simmer and cook for 10 minutes or until the lamb is cooked, then season to taste with salt and pepper and stir through the pistachios (if using) and lemon juice.

7. Remove the aubergine halves from the oven once soft, divide among plates and pile the spiced lamb on top. Scatter with mint and drizzle over some yoghurt.

✳ Use It Up

You can use minced beef or any other mince here instead of lamb. For a meat-free version of this dish, swap the lamb for quinoa or lentils.

Spiced lamb chops with mint oil

This makes a quick yet still hearty alternative to a Sunday roast. Lamb chops are delightfully fast to cook under the grill and they're also perfect for the family as you can adjust the level of spice that you add to each chop, so that everyone is happy. See p. 125 for a homemade spice mix, or use a shop-bought paste. The mint oil makes a perfect flavour pairing with the lamb. Serve with watercress and Cauliflower Mash (p. 274), as pictured here.

Serves 4

8 small lamb chops
1 tablespoon harissa spice mix
  (see Use It Up)

MINT OIL
1 handful of fresh mint leaves,
  roughly chopped
5 tablespoons extra-virgin
  olive oil
2 tablespoons apple cider
  vinegar
2 teaspoons raw honey
Sea salt and black pepper

TO SERVE
Caulflower mash (p. 274)
200g watercress, roughly torn
1 small handful of chopped
  pistachios or flaked almonds
  (optional)
1 small handful mint leaves,
  roughly torn

1. Make the mint oil by whisking all the ingredients together in a small bowl. Season to taste with salt and pepper and set aside.

2. Preheat the grill to high. Place the lamb chops on a tray. Rub the harissa spice and some salt and pepper into the lamb and grill for 3–5 minutes on each side (depending how rare you like them), then leave to rest for 5 minutes.

3. While the lamb is grilling then resting, make the cauliflower mash. Divide the cauliflower mash, made with added feta, among the plates. Toss the watercress in the mint dressing and add a big pile to each plate. Place the chops on top, with a few pistachios, almonds or torn mint leaves sprinkled over, if you like. Serve.

Sausage & kale tray bake with mustard drizzle

This cosy, comforting dish brings together some perfect sausage pairings – sage, mustard and apples. Use chipolata sausages or regular sausages cut into quarters. This would also be delicious made with lamb merguez sausages, though you could include any type of sausage. Serve it with a big green crunchy salad tossed in an apple cider vinegar dressing or with a bowl of Carrot Mash (p. 274) or Butter Bean Mash (p. 198).

Serves 4

1 tablespoon coconut oil
   or ghee
1 celeriac (800g), peeled
   and cut into 1.5cm cubes
1 red onion or large leek,
   roughly sliced
1 large red pepper, deseeded
   and roughly chopped
1 apple (such as Cox or
   Braeburn), cored and
   roughly chopped
6 regular sausages, quartered,
   or 12 chipolatas (total 400g)
1 tablespoon chopped fresh
   rosemary or 1 teaspoon
   dried rosemary
200g kale, chopped
Sea salt and black pepper

MUSTARD DRIZZLE
12 fresh sage leaves, finely
   chopped
3 tablespoons mustard
   (or to taste)
1½ tablespoons maple syrup
1 tablespoon apple cider
   vinegar
2 tablespoons extra-virgin
   olive oil

1. Preheat the oven to fan 220°C/Gas mark 9. Add the oil to a large baking tray or ovenproof dish and leave in the oven for a few minutes to melt.

2. Add all the vegetables (apart from the kale) to the tray with the apple, sausages and herbs. Season with salt and pepper and toss in the hot oil, then spread everything out in a single layer, with the sausages on top, and roast in the oven for 18 minutes.

3. Meanwhile, whisk all the ingredients for the mustard drizzle in a bowl and season with salt and pepper.

4. Remove the tray from the oven and add the kale. Toss everything together and place back in the oven to bake for a further 8–10 minutes until the sausages are cooked through and golden brown and the celeriac is tender. Pour over the mustard drizzle and then to serve.

Filipino-style steak & onions

This is the Filipino version of steak and onions, known as *bisteak*. My mum grew up in Manila cooking it with *kalamansi*, a cross between a mandarin and a kumquat, but lemon makes a good substitute. This dish takes less than 10 minutes to cook, freeing up time to make a great side or two. Try Cauliflower or Broccoli Rice (p. 272) and maybe some Killer Kale (p. 201) or a load of lightly cooked spinach.

Serves 4

2 tablespoons coconut oil
  or ghee
2 large onions, sliced
  into rings
500g sirloin steak,
  cut into 5mm slices
1 tablespoon chickpea flour
3 garlic cloves, finely chopped
Juice of 1 lemon
4 tablespoons tamari
Sea salt and black pepper

1. Melt half the oil in a large, wide frying pan, add the onion rings and fry over a low-medium heat for about 3 minutes until softened slightly but still with a bit of bite, then set aside on a plate.

2. Dust the steak slices in flour and season with a little salt and pepper.

3. Melt the remaining oil in the same pan, add the steak pieces, in batches if necessary, and fry over a high heat for about 1 minute on each side, then transfer to the plate with the onion rings.

4. Fry the garlic in the pan for about 30 seconds. Add the lemon juice, tamari and a good pinch of pepper and simmer for 2 minutes.

5. Return the steak and onions to the pan to gently heat through for 30 seconds and then serve.

Mamma mia meatballs

There is so much variety when it comes to pasta these days. You could serve this with quinoa spaghetti, buckwheat pasta or mung bean noodles, for instance. It would also work welll with spiralized raw courgettes or celeriac (p. 273). The grated carrots add sweetness to the meatballs, sneaking in some extra veg while helping the meat to go a bit further. The meatballs freeze well, so why not make a double batch and freeze half raw. As both the meatballs and sauce use onions and garlic, you effectively save a step by frying it all up to begin with.

Serves 4

2½ tablespoons butter or ghee
1 large onion, finely chopped
  (see time saver)
4 garlic cloves, finely chopped
1 large carrot, roughly grated
1 egg
500g minced beef, or any meat
1 tablespoon dried oregano
½ teaspoon chilli flakes
2 tablespoons tomato purée
2 x 400g tins of chopped
  tomatoes
Sea salt and black pepper

TO SERVE
1 large handful of fresh basil
  leaves, torn
2 handfuls of grated Parmesan

1. Melt 1½ tablespoons of butter in a large pan, add the onions and fry over a medium-low heat for 5 minutes until softened, stirring occasionally. Add the garlic and fry for 1 minute.

2. Meanwhile, place the carrot in a large bowl, add the egg, beef, oregano, chilli flakes and ½ teaspoon each of salt and pepper. At this point, add half of the fried onion and garlic mixture to the bowl.

3. To make the tomato sauce, add the tomato purée to the remaining onion/garlic mixture in the pan. Tip in the tinned tomatoes, season with salt and pepper and bring to the boil. Reduce the heat slightly and leave the sauce to simmer over a medium-high heat for 10–12 minutes to thicken and reduce.

4. Meanwhile, combine the meat mixture and, with damp hands, form into 24 bite-sized meatballs. (An easy way to do this is to split the mixture into four and then divide each piece into six.)

5. Melt the remaining butter in a large frying pan, add the meatballs and fry on a medium-high heat for 6 minutes, shaking the pan halfway through, until browned all over.

6. Tip the meatballs into the tomato sauce pan and simmer, covered with a lid, on a medium heat for 10 minutes until the meatballs are cooked through. Use this time to make your choice of pasta or noodles then toss everything together and serve with basil leaves and let everyone help themselves to Parmesan.

••●• Time Saver

*To save time, simply whizz up the onion and garlic in
a food processor.*

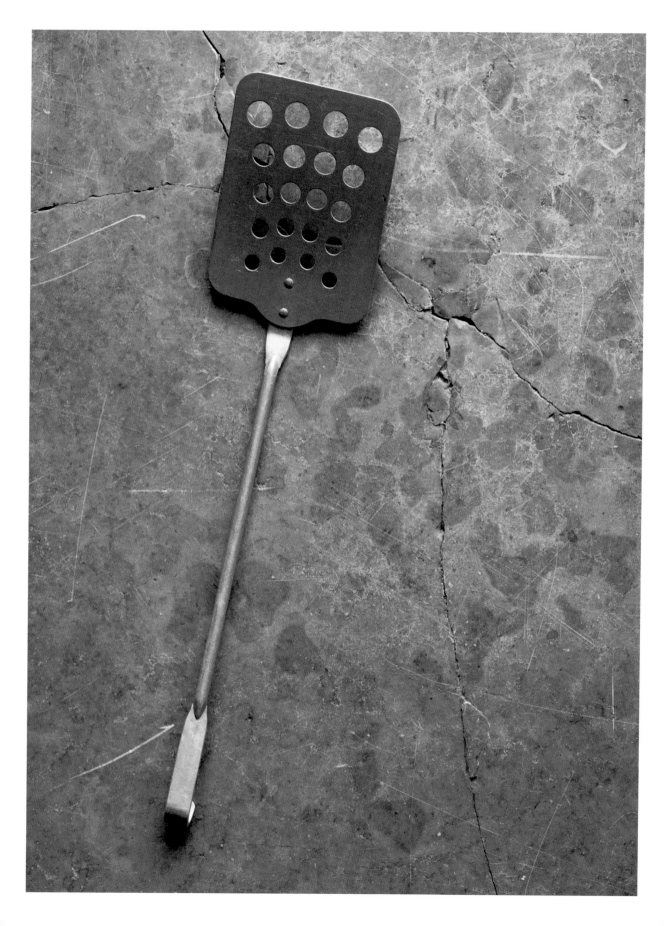

FISH

'Whether grilled, baked or fried, fish makes for the ideal 30-minute meal. There is such a range to choose from, whether white fish such as coley, cod, pollock or sea bass, or omega-3-rich oily fish like salmon or the much cheaper mackerel, sardines or anchovies. Although specific types of fish are mentioned in many of the recipes, every one of them can be adjusted to cook with other kinds of fish. You just need to adapt the cooking times slightly depending on the thickness of the fillet or the type. When buying fish, follow your fishmonger's recommendations for what's best – what's sustainable and good value – as this can change from day to day. '

If you're new to cooking fish, give the fishcakes a go (p. 116), which use tinned sardines and cauliflower mash; they are inexpensive and quick to make. Salmon is always very straightforward to cook and, with its firm, rich texture, very satisfying too. For the easiest of meals that every member of the family will like, you can't beat the Sesame Salmon & Miso Veg Tray Bake (p. 126), all cooked in one tray and full of goodness and familiar flavours.

I love the Thai Cauliflower Fried Rice with Prawns (p. 112), bursting with spicy flavours, and texture, or the super-speedy Garlic Tapas Prawns (p. 118), ready in just 5 minutes and perfect for a summery starter.

For quick weeknight meals, I tend to use fillets instead of whole fish as they are available to buy in most supermarkets that don't have a dedicated fish counter, plus they're easier to keep an eye on when cooking. Two of my favourites are Five-Spice Sea Bass on p. 121 or the Grilled Mullet with Greek Salad on p. 117. Don't feel that you have to buy the precise type of fish that each recipe calls for, any variety will work well and you must try the Ginger Fish Burgers on p. 114 – incredible served with hoisin sauce and sprinkled with sesame seeds and fresh coriander.

This chapter includes some other really tasty sauces, which can make all the difference to a dish. Check out the Jalapeño Salsa (p. 113) or Teriyaki Sauce (p. 128) – either of which would be great drizzled over any kind of vegetables. Another favourite is the Wasabi Pea Dip (p. 110), which accompanies my take on fish and chips – Japanese-style! But it would go beautifully with the Chickpea Crackers on p. 212 as a snack or party canapé.

For more fish recipes try:

NYC-style Big Blinis
    Breakfast & Brunch (p. 38)

Hot-smoked Trout with a Beetroot Fennel Salad & Scandi-Style Dressing
    Salads (p. 178)

Smoked Mackerel Pâté
    Breakfast & Brunch (p. 24)

Smoked Mackerel and Jalapeño Salsa Tacos
    Breakfast & Brunch (p. 32)

Spinach & Smoked Trout Muffins
    Breakfast & Brunch (p. 25)

Meat/fish swaps

Try swapping meat for fish in the following recipes:

Beef & Carrot Koftas (p. 94)
Pulse any firm fish, combine with the kofta ingredients and bake
for about 10 minutes.

Chicken Fajitas (p. 82)
Use salmon instead and fry for about 5 minutes until cooked through.

Chicken Goujons (p. 82)
Replace with any firm white fish and bake for about 12 minutes.

Easy Chicken & Tomato Curry (p. 84)
Swap with chunks of any firm fish and add in the last 8–10 mins of cooking.

Italian Chicken Stew (p. 81)
Swap with chunks of cod and add in the last 8–10 minutes of cooking.

Japanese fish with wasabi pea dip

Serve this with Butternut Squash Fries (p. 206) for fish and chips, Japanese-style! The wasabi pea dip is so tasty that I make it all the time as a snack and serve it with Chickpea Crackers (p. 212). If you want to change this recipe up, you could omit the sesame seeds and swap the wasabi for some capers and cornichons to make tartare sauce instead. Any white fish fillets will do here, such as cod, coley, haddock or pollock, and you could chop them into smaller pieces for baked goujons (fish fingers). This would also go well with Quickly Pickled Veg (p. 199) and Spiced Ketchup (p. 206) as pictured here.

Serves 4

90g ground almonds
1½ tablespoons sesame seeds,
  plus extra for sprinkling
¼ teaspoon cayenne pepper
1 egg
4 skinless firm white fish
  fillets (total 600g)
2 teaspoons toasted sesame oil
Sea salt and black pepper
1 lime, cut into wedges,
  to serve

WASABI PEA DIP
120g frozen peas, thawed
1½ teaspoons wasabi powder
  (or to taste)
Flesh of 1 avocado
2 tablespoons natural yoghurt
Juice of 1 lime
1 tablespoon tamari

1. Preheat the oven to fan 220°C/Gas mark 9 and line a baking tray with baking parchment. If making the squash fries too, pop them on a second baking tray and follow the instructions on p. 206.

2. Mix the ground almonds, sesame seeds and cayenne pepper in a shallow bowl, then beat the egg in another bowl and season with salt and pepper.

3. Dip the fish first in egg and then in the ground almond/sesame seed mix, making sure that the fillets are fully coated. Place on the prepared tray and sprinkle each with a tiny drizzle of toasted sesame oil.

4. Bake in the oven for 10–12 minutes until golden brown and cooked through.

5. Meanwhile, make the dip. Place the peas in a food processor with all the other ingredients and pulse briefly or a bit longer for a smoother texture, if you prefer. (I like this to have the texture of mushy peas.) Taste for seasoning, adding a pinch of salt if you like.

6. Plate up the fish, sprinkle with sesame seeds and serve with the lime wedges and the wasabi pea dip on the side.

✳ Use It Up

You can replace the wasabi with a 3cm piece of finely chopped or grated ginger.

Thai cauliflower fried 'rice' with prawns

This simple stir-fry is full of punchy Thai flavours. Don't worry if you haven't got lemongrass to hand; just make sure you've got plenty of garlic and ginger. I recommend using a food processor here to make light work of chopping all the ingredients, but you can chop everything by hand if you prefer. Frozen peas are so useful to keep in the freezer, and you could use frozen prawns here too, if you like. Frozen prawns will need defrosting for a few hours.

Serves 4

1 onion, quartered
3 garlic cloves, peeled
3cm piece of ginger
1 fresh red chilli, deseeded
1 lemongrass stalk (tough
    outer leaves removed)
1 cauliflower (total 900g)
2 tablespoons coconut oil
300g peeled raw prawns
3 handfuls of frozen peas
3 eggs
2 tablespoons tamari
2 tablespoons fish sauce
Sea salt and black pepper

TO SERVE
1 large handful of fresh
    coriander or Thai basil
    leaves, roughly torn
1 lime, cut into wedges
1 handful of cashew nuts
    or peanuts, toasted
    and chopped

1. Use a food processor to blitz the onion, garlic, ginger, chilli and lemongrass, then transfer to a small bowl. Follow the instructions on p. 272 to grate or process the cauliflowers into 'rice'. (There is no need to wash out the food processor bowl first, if using.)

2. Melt half the oil in a saucepan, add the prawns and a pinch of salt and fry on a high heat for about 1 minute until they change from grey to pink, then transfer to another bowl and set aside.

3. Put the pan straight back on the heat and add the remaining oil. When the oil has melted, tip in the blitzed onion mix and fry for 30 seconds, then add the cauliflower rice and cook on a high heat for 3 minutes, stirring occasionally, adding a splash of water if it's catching on the base of the pan. Stir in the frozen peas and cook for 1 more minute.

4. Push everything to one side of the pan and crack the eggs quickly into the empty part of the pan. Let the eggs start to cook and set over a high heat for about 30 seconds, then season with a little salt and pepper and roughly scramble for another 30 seconds until just cooked.

5. Return the prawns to the pan, add the tamari and fish sauce and stir everything together. Remove from the heat, taste for seasoning and sprinkle over the fresh herbs. Serve with the lime wedges and scattered with the toasted chopped nuts.

✳ Use It Up

You could use cooked prawns or 200g cooked flaked fish, or swap for 1 large chopped aubergine or 300g mushrooms and make this an all-vegetable dish.

Baked hake with jalapeño salsa

Hake works really well with these Mexican-spiced vegetables and jalapeño salsa. The salsa is amazing with fried eggs, drizzled over roasted cauliflower or broccoli or served with Chicken Fajitas (p. 82). Butter Bean Mash (p. 198) would be perfect with this, or serve with a slaw (p. 177) or a simple green salad for a refreshing crunchy addition.

Serves 4

1½ tablespoons coconut oil
   or ghee
1 large cauliflower
   (about 900g), chopped into
   equal-sized florets
2 peppers, deseeded and sliced
300g cherry tomatoes
1 teaspoon smoked paprika
½ teaspoon cayenne pepper
   (or to taste)
4 large hake fillets (total 700g)
1 lime, thinly sliced into
   8 rounds
Sea salt and black pepper
Flesh of 1 large avocado, sliced,
   to serve

JALAPEÑO SALSA
2 garlic cloves, finely chopped
1–2 jalapeños, deseeded and
   finely chopped (or to taste)
1 large handful of fresh
   coriander, finely chopped
Juice and grated zest of 1 lime
4 tablespoons extra-virgin
   olive oil
1 teaspoon raw honey or
   maple syrup (optional)

1. Preheat the oven to fan 220°C/Gas mark 9. Add the oil to a large baking tray and pop in the oven for a few minutes for the oil to melt.

2. Remove the tray from the oven and add all the vegetables. Sprinkle over the smoked paprika, cayenne pepper and some salt and pepper and carefully toss everything together in the melted oil. Spread out in a single layer and roast in the oven for 18 minutes.

3. Meanwhile, mix together all the ingredients for the salsa, seasoning to taste with salt and pepper.

4. Remove the tray from the oven, toss the vegetables and spread out in a single layer again. Place the fish fillets on top of the vegetables, sprinkle with salt and pepper and cover with the lime slices. Put back in the oven to cook for 8–10 minutes until the fish is just cooked through.

5. Divide the roasted veg among plates and lay a hake fillet on top of each. Serve with the sliced avocado and lots of salsa spooned over.

••●• Time Saver

You can save a bit of chopping time by pulsing the garlic, jalapeños and coriander in a food processor, then mixing in the liquid ingredients.

Ginger fish burgers

You can use any good-quality fish for this recipe, from trout and salmon to hake, cod and coley – whatever is sustainably sourced and in season. You could serve these burgers in lettuce wraps or with a salad, such as the Herb & Pak Choi Salad (p. 171) as pictured here. They would also go well with Vegetable Rice (p. 272) or noodles, and would be excellent eaten cold the next day as part of a packed lunch. If you fall in love with the hoisin sauce, like me, try the Duck Pancakes (p. 92).

Serves 4

4 fish fillets (total 700g),
   skinned and any little
   bones removed
2 garlic cloves, peeled
3cm piece of ginger
4 spring onions, sliced
1 small handful of fresh
   coriander
2 tablespoons tamari
¼ teaspoon sea salt
1 teaspoon chilli flakes (or to
   taste), plus extra to serve
Grated zest of 1 lime
1 tablespoon coconut oil
   or ghee

TO SERVE
1 quantity of hoisin sauce
   (p. 92)
1 tablespoon sesame seeds
1 handful of fresh coriander
   or mint leaves (optional)
A few heads of Gem lettuce,
   leaves separated

1. Place the fish in a food processor and pulse a few times. Add all the other ingredients (except the oil) and pulse again a few times.

2. Form the mixture into four burgers, about 10cm wide and 2cm thick (or make 8 smaller burgers), then chill in the fridge for 5–10 minutes, if you have time, to firm up (this makes them easier to fry). Meanwhile, make the sauce (p. 92).

3. Melt the oil in a large frying pan over a medium-high heat and fry the burgers on one side for 3 minutes, pressing down to flatten and get nicely browned underneath. Flip over to fry on the other side for 3 minutes until browned and just cooked through.

4. Quickly add the hoisin sauce to the pan to heat through for 1 minute (or use a fresh pan), then serve alongside the burgers. Serve the burgers in lettuce leaves, as pictured here. Sprinkle over more chilli flakes and scatter with the sesame seeds and coriander leaves, if you like.

● Tip

The burgers are best pan-fried, but you could also griddle, barbecue or bake them for 10–15 minutes at fan 190°C/Gas mark 6½.

Sardine fishcakes with pea & rocket salad

Sardines are such a great store cupboard staple – healthy, inexpensive and so easy to use. I've paired them here with cauliflower mash to make into these simple and very delicious fishcakes. The fishcakes are served with a fresh pea and rocket salad, but they would also go well with a poached egg and spinach. You could also add extra herbs and spices to the fishcake mix, such as a teaspoon of harissa or some garam masala, chilli and chopped coriander.

Serves 4 /
Makes 12 fishcakes

1 quantity of cauliflower mash
   (p. 274)
2 x 120g tins of sardines in
   olive oil, drained
1 handful of fresh parsley or
   dill, roughly chopped
1 egg, beaten
4 tablespoons flour (such as
   ground almond, buckwheat
   or chickpea)
2 tablespoons capers (optional)
1½ tablespoons coconut oil
   or ghee
Sea salt and black pepper
1 lemon, cut into wedges
   to serve

PEA AND ROCKET SALAD
100g rocket
1 large handful of fresh or
   frozen peas (see Time Saver)
2 tablespoons extra-virgin
   olive oil
1 tablespoon lemon juice
Sea salt and black pepper

1. Place the cauliflower mash in a large bowl. (If it is freshly made, rather than firm from the fridge, briefly heat through in a pan to remove any excess liquid.)

2. Mash the sardines with a fork and add to the cauliflower mash with the herbs, egg, flour and capers (if using) and combine well. Season with pepper and taste before adding any salt (as sardines are salty), then divide the mixture into 12 portions. Use damp hands to shape each portion into a fishcake about 2cm thick and 6cm wide.

3. Melt the oil in a large, wide frying pan. Add six fishcakes (or as many as you can comfortably fit in your pan) and fry on a medium heat for 3 minutes, then flip over and fry for another 2–3 minutes until golden brown on each side. Repeat with the remaining fishcakes, keeping the first batch warm in a low oven.

4. Place the rocket in a serving bowl and add the peas. Dress with the olive oil, lemon juice and a little sea salt and black pepper and serve with the fishcakes and lemon wedges.

••●• Time Saver

If using frozen peas, pour over a little hot water to defrost them, and then drain.

● Tip

Swap the sardines for another type of tinned fish, or use 150g cooked flaked fish, such as smoked mackerel or hot-smoked salmon or trout. Always try to get your fish from sustainable sources, if you can.

Grilled mullet with Greek salad

Spring onions and lettuce wedges are delicious grilled – just keep your eye on them so they don't burn! This would be delicious with whole mullet on a barbecue or you could pan-fry the fillets with the lettuce and spring onions. Chop the salad ingredients chunkily and make extra so you can have the leftovers to enjoy the next day with some lentils or quinoa in a Waste Not, Want Not Bowl (p. 72).

Serves 4

1½ tablespoon ghee
4 large grey mullet fillets
   (total 700g)
4 spring onions, halved
   lengthways if large
4 Little Gem lettuces, sliced
   into wedges
1 tablespoon roughly chopped
   fresh thyme or oregano
   leaves
Sea salt and black pepper
A squeeze of lemon, to serve

GREEK SALAD
1 small red onion, thinly sliced
Juice of ½ lemon
1 large red pepper, deseeded
   and cut into chunks
3 tomatoes, quartered, or 200g
   cherry tomatoes, halved
1 cucumber, roughly chopped
1 handful of pitted
   olives, halved
1 large handful of fresh
   parsley, roughly chopped
1 teaspoon dried oregano
   or thyme
150g feta, roughly crumbled
6 tablespoons extra-virgin
   olive oil
Sea salt and black pepper

1. Preheat the grill to high. Add the ghee to a baking tray and pop in the oven for a few minutes for the ghee to melt.

2. Meanwhile, prepare the salad. Place the sliced red onion with the lemon juice in a large salad bowl, so it has a chance to soften, and add the pepper, tomatoes, cucumber, olives, herbs and half the feta, but don't mix yet.

3. Remove the tray from the grill and add the fish with the spring onions and lettuce wedges. Sprinkle with salt, pepper and fresh herbs and toss gently in the melted ghee. Spread everything out on the tray and grill for 4–5 minutes until the fish is just cooked through and the lettuce and spring onions are golden.

4. Add the olive oil to the salad, season with a little sea salt and black pepper, then toss all the ingredients together and top with the remaining feta.

5. Divide the fish, lettuce and spring onions among plates, squeeze over a little lemon juice and serve with the Greek salad.

Garlic tapas prawns

A taste of Spanish summer in just 5 minutes. Look for prawns in the shell, if your guests will like these, or buy the peeled ones for ease. They can be served hot or cold, and as a starter or a side. You could turn them into a sort of prawn cocktail with lettuce, avocado and Garlic Yoghurt Dressing (p. 183) or add them to the Salsa Salad (p.176) or California-style Kale Salad (p. 174) or just serve simply with little Gem lettuce dressed with olive oil and balsamic vinegar as pictured here.

Serves 4 as a starter or side

1 tablespoon butter or ghee
3 large garlic cloves, finely sliced
1 fresh red chilli, deseeded and finely chopped (or to taste)
300g raw prawns (or 500g with heads and tails on)
¼ teaspoon smoked paprika
A pinch of sea salt
2 tablespoons white wine or dry sherry
1 small handful of fresh parsley, chopped, to serve
Little Gem lettuce, to serve

1. Melt the butter in a wide frying pan, add the garlic and chilli and gently fry on a medium heat for 1 minute until the garlic is softened but not browned.

2. Turn up the heat, add the prawns, paprika and salt and fry for 30 seconds, then add the wine or sherry and cook for another 1 minute until the prawns turn pink.

3. Serve with a sprinkling of chopped parsley and extra salt.

✱ Use It Up

You can replace the wine or sherry with 1½ tablespoons of lemon juice.

Keralan turmeric fish curry

A mildly spiced south Indian curry, naturally sweetened by the creamy coconut, this is great with any firm white fish and would work well with other seafood too. Make it without the curry leaves or mustard seeds, if you can't get them easily, and serve with Vegetable Rice (p. 272) or naans (p. 191). I like this curry to be rich and coconut-flavoured, so I've used one and a half tins of coconut milk, but you could replace the half-tin with stock or broth instead.

Serves 4

1½ teaspoons mustard seeds
1 tablespoon coconut oil
  or ghee
1 large onion, thinly sliced
1 fresh chilli, deseeded and
  finely chopped (or to taste)
1 teaspoon ground turmeric
7 curry leaves (dried or fresh)
3cm piece of ginger, finely
  chopped
4 garlic cloves, finely chopped
1½ x 400ml tins of coconut
  milk (total 600ml)
2 handfuls of fresh
  coriander stalks and leaves,
  finely chopped
700g firm white fish (such as
  pollock or coley)
Sea salt and black pepper
1 lime, cut into wedges,
  to serve

1. Fry the mustard seeds in a large, wide, dry pan over a medium heat until they start to jump (after about 30 seconds), then add the oil. When the oil has melted, add the onions and fry for 6 minutes to soften, stirring occasionally.

2. Add the chilli, turmeric and curry leaves with the ginger and garlic, and fry for another 3 minutes, stirring halfway through. Add a splash of water if the mixture starts to catch.

3. Add the coconut milk and coriander stalks, and season with salt and pepper, then bring to a medium simmer and cook for 10 minutes, uncovered.

4. Meanwhile, slice the fish into 2.5cm cubes and add to the curry to simmer for 4–5 minutes until cooked through. Remove from the heat, then squeeze in the juice of one of the lime wedges, season to taste, scatter over the coriander leaves and serve with the remaining lime wedges.

✳ Use It Up

Put the rest of the coconut milk to good use by adding it to smoothies, shakes, soups and stews, e.g. Big Batch Dhal (p. 51).

Five-spice sea bass

Chinese five-spice powder is a gorgeous blend of cinnamon, cloves, fennel seeds, star anise and Sichuan pepper. You only need a little to add a lovely touch of aromatic flavour in savoury recipes, as well as in baking or for poaching fruit. Serve this with your choice of side, like the Sesame Carrot & Courgette Noodles (p. 164) or the Ginger, Garlic, Pak Choi & Mushrooms (p. 199).

Serves 4

2 teaspoons coconut oil
or ghee
4 fillets of sea bass (total 700g)
1 teaspoon Chinese five-spice
powder
1 teaspoon chilli flakes
(or to taste)
2 teaspoons tamari
Sea salt and black pepper

TO SERVE
1 tablespoon chives, chopped
Lemon or lime wedges

1. Preheat the grill to high. Add the oil to a baking tray and leave under the grill for a few minutes for the oil to melt.

2. Place the sea bass fillets on the baking tray, sprinkle over the spices, tamari and a little salt and pepper (bearing in mind that tamari is salty) and gently toss in the melted oil. Lay the fish, skin side up, in the tray and grill for 3–4 minutes until cooked through and the skin is crispy.

3. Serve sprinkled with the chives and with lemon or lime wedges for squeezing over.

✳ Use It Up

Enjoy this recipe with the 'catch of the day' from the fishmonger. This is a great way to try new types of fish at an affordable price.

Fish en papillote

It has a fancy name, but these are actually very simple fish parcels made with baking parchment and wrapped to seal in the flavours and juices. This is one of the easiest ways to cook fish and any firm white fillets will do, such as haddock, cod, coley or halibut. The pesto drizzled over at the end really makes the dish, but you could try another sauce to completely change the flavour, such as Mexican-style Jalapeño Salsa (p. 113) or Filipino-style Tamarind Sauce (p. 131). Serve with a green salad or Vegetable Mash (p. 274).

Serves 2

200g green beans, trimmed
 and halved
2 firm white fish fillets (total
 300g)
16 cherry tomatoes, halved
2 teaspoons butter or ghee,
 melted
1½ teaspoons dried thyme
½ lemon, sliced into rounds
Sea salt and black pepper
½ quantity of pesto (p. 67)
 or 3 tablespoons of shop-
 bought pesto, to serve

1. Preheat the oven to fan 200°C/Gas mark 7 and cut two sheets of baking parchment, each about 20cm long.

2. Place a pile of beans in the middle of each sheet of paper. Place a fish fillet on top of each pile of beans and scatter the cherry tomatoes around.

3. Rub the top of the fish with the melted butter, then sprinkle the herbs over the tomatoes and fish and season with salt and pepper. Place the lemon slices on top of the fish and bring two sides of the paper together, folding over in the middle and scrunching the open ends to seal. Repeat for both parcels.

4. Place on a baking tray and cook in the oven for 8–12 minutes (depending on the thickness of the fillets and the type of fish). Remove from the oven and allow to rest for a minute before opening the parcels. Use this time to make the pesto.

5. Transfer the contents of each parcel to a plate, then drizzle with the juices and spoon the pesto over the fish to serve.

✳ Use It Up

Swap the green beans for Tenderstem broccoli or asparagus and swap thyme for oregano or rosemary, dried or fresh.

Harissa fish with herby cauliflower couscous

The cherry tomatoes and fish are coated in harissa and roasted, then served with a cooling, herby cauliflower couscous, which offsets the spicy heat. Anyone who is unsure about cauliflower will be converted by this delicious side dish. Mixing your own harissa is simple, with the advantage that you can adjust the level of chilli, though for speed you could use 1 tablespoon of a quality harissa spice mix or paste. I like to roast up extra tomatoes and keep them in the fridge, ready to add a burst of colour and flavour to a Waste Not, Want Not Bowl (p. 72).

Serves 2

1½ tablespoons coconut oil
  or ghee
200g cherry tomatoes on
  the vine
2 large firm white fish fillets
  (such as sea bream or hake;
  total 300g)

HARISSA SPICES
1 teaspoon caraway seeds or
  smoked paprika
1 teaspoon ground cumin
1 teaspoon ground coriander
A pinch of cayenne pepper
1 teaspoon dried mint or
  thyme
Sea salt and black pepper

CAULIFLOWER COUSCOUS
2 teaspoons coconut oil
  or ghee
1 garlic clove, finely chopped
1 large cauliflower (900g)
Juice and grated zest of
  ½ lemon, plus lemon
  wedges to serve
2 large handfuls of mixed
  fresh herbs (coriander,
  parsley or dill), chopped

OPTIONAL EXTRAS
1 handful of mixed seeds or
  chopped nuts
1 handful of dried fruit

1. Preheat the oven to fan 220°C/Gas mark 9.

2. Sprinkle the harissa spices and herbs on a baking tray, add the oil and place in the oven for a few minutes to allow the oil to melt.

3. Remove the tray from the oven and carefully toss the tomatoes in the melted oil and spices, then return to the oven to roast for 12 minutes.

4. Meanwhile, follow the instructions on p. 272 to grate or process the cauliflower into 'rice'.

5. Remove the baking tray from the oven, pushing the cherry tomatoes to one side of the tray. Carefully rub both sides of the fish fillets in the hot spiced oil, then lay, skin side up, and roast in the oven for 5–8 minutes until cooked through. (Timing will depend on the thickness of each fillet and the type of fish.)

6. Meanwhile, make the cauliflower couscous. Melt the oil in a large pan, add the garlic and fry for 30 seconds, then tip in the cauliflower 'rice', turn up the heat and fry for 3–4 minutes until just cooked through, stirring occasionally. Remove from the heat, then add the lemon juice and zest, season with salt and pepper and mix in the fresh herbs and any optional extras.

7. Plate up the cauliflower rice, top with the roasted cherry tomatoes and fish fillets, and serve with a wedge of lemon.

Sesame salmon & miso veg tray bake

A real winner of a dish, this is one I make on rotation, using any leftovers in a packed lunch. Miso is both nourishing and delicious; it's an expensive ingredient but you only need a couple of tablespoons here. Serve with a big handful of crunchy and refreshing salad leaves, such as watercress dressed in a little lime or lemon juice. Try this with the Quickly Pickled Veg (p. 199).

Serves 2

1 tablespoon coconut oil
 or ghee
1 large aubergine, cut
 vertically into quarters
2 large courgettes, cut
 vertically into quarters
2 salmon fillets (total 300g)
1 teaspoon toasted sesame oil
1 tablespoon mixed black and
 white sesame seeds
Sea salt and black pepper

MISO GINGER SAUCE
Juice of 1 lime
1 tablespoon maple syrup
3cm piece of ginger, grated
2 tablespoons miso paste
2 tablespoons hot water

TO SERVE
2 spring onions, sliced
1 handful of fresh coriander,
 stalks and leaves finely
 chopped
Chilli flakes, to taste

1. Preheat the oven to fan 220°C/Gas mark 9. Add the oil to a baking tray and place in the oven for a few minutes for the oil to melt.

2. Place the aubergine and courgette slices on the baking tray, season with salt and pepper and toss in the melted oil. Spread the vegetable slices on the tray, skin side down and in a single layer, and bake in the oven for 15 minutes.

3. Meanwhile, mix together all the ingredients for the miso ginger sauce in a small bowl.

4. Remove the tray from the oven, toss everything together and drizzle the miso ginger sauce over the vegetables. Nestle the salmon, skin side down, among the vegetables and drizzle over the toasted sesame oil. Season the salmon with salt and pepper and sprinkle over the sesame seeds, then roast in the oven for 8–10 minutes until the fillets are just cooked through and the vegetables are tender.

5. Serve sprinkled with the spring onions, coriander and chilli.

✳ Use It Up

Swap the courgette for Tenderstem broccoli or asparagus and swap lime for orange or lemon if you have some that need eating.

Spicy salmon teriyaki

A 10-minute recipe that everyone loves. It's perfect with salmon but you can use any fish fillets you like; just check with your fishmonger as cooking times may vary. You can serve this with different sides, such as the really quick Broccoli Rice (p. 272) as pictured here, leftover quinoa or & Mushrooms (p. 199). The sauce is also great with chicken, fried aubergines or drizzled over roasted squash or cauliflower. I recommend making extra and keeping it to jazz up stir-fries and noodles during the week.

Serves 4

1 tablespoon coconut oil
 or ghee
4 wild salmon fillets
 (total 700g)
Sea salt and black pepper

TERIYAKI SAUCE
2 garlic cloves, finely chopped
3cm piece of ginger, finely
 chopped
1 teaspoon chilli flakes
 (or to taste)
4 tablespoons tamari
Juice of ½ lemon or lime
1½ tablespoons maple syrup

TO SERVE
Broccoli Rice (p. 272)
2 spring onions, sliced
Grated zest of 1 lemon or lime
Chilli flakes (optional)

1. Whisk the sauce ingredients together in a bowl. Alternatively, whizz in a high-powered blender if you prefer (in which case you don't need to finely chop the garlic and ginger). Make the broccoli rice if using, or your choice of side.

2. Melt the oil in a wide frying pan. Season the salmon with salt and pepper, add to the pan and fry, skin side down, over a high heat for 1 minute to make the skin crispy.

3. Flip the fillets over, so they are skin side up, and pour in the sauce (avoiding the skin so it stays crispy). Simmer over a medium heat for 2–3 minutes until the sauce is hot and the salmon is just cooked through.

4. Divide the rice among the plates, top with salmon, then sprinkle over the spring onions, lemon or lime zest and chilli flakes (if using) to serve.

✳ Use It Up

Swap broccoli for cauliflower.

Grilled mackerel with tamarind ginger greens

Tamarind is what makes the sauce for Asian dishes like Pad Thai (p. 136) taste so good, and this dish is inspired by my Filipino Mum who loves tamarind and always fed it to me as a child. Its tangy sweet-sour flavour perfectly cuts through the oily mackerel, which you could swap with another type of fish fillet, or use whole fish instead. The ginger greens are lovely hot or warm, or eaten cold as a salad. You can swap in any green veg you have in the fridge.

Serves 4

1 teaspoon coconut oil or ghee
8 mackerel fillets (total 700g)
Sea salt and black pepper

FILIPINO-STYLE
TAMARIND SAUCE
3 tablespoons tamarind paste
1 teaspoon chilli flakes, (or to taste)
1 tablespoon maple syrup
2 tablespoons tamari
Juice of 1 lime

GREENS
1½ tablespoons coconut oil or ghee
4 spring onions, sliced (green parts saved to garnish)
3 garlic cloves, finely chopped
3cm piece of ginger, finely chopped
1 head of broccoli (about 300g), cut into small florets
250g green beans, trimmed
250g sugar snap peas or mangetout, chopped

TO SERVE
1 large handful of mixed fresh herbs (such as coriander, basil or mint), finely chopped
1 large handful of cashews, toasted and roughly chopped

1. Preheat the grill to high. Add the oil to a baking tray and pop under the grill for a few minutes to melt.

2. Whisk the sauce ingredients in a bowl and set aside. Toast the nuts in a dry saucepan and then set aside.

3. For the greens, melt the 1½ tablespoons of oil in the saucepan, add the white parts of the spring onions, garlic and ginger and fry over a medium heat for 30 seconds.

4. Tip in all the green vegetables and stir-fry for 5 minutes until just tender. Add a splash of water if the greens are getting too dry and sticking to the pan.

5. Meanwhile, place the mackerel fillets on the greased baking tray, skin side up, season with salt and pepper then grill for 4–5 minutes until just cooked through.

6. When the greens are just tender, pour in the tamarind sauce and stir in. Increase the heat and simmer for about 30 seconds to heat through. Taste for seasoning, adding a little more tamari if you'd like it to be saltier.

7. Serve the greens with the fish, scattered with the green parts of the spring onions and the fresh herbs and toasted nuts.

VEGETABLE MAINS

'THE vast majority of the recipes in this book are based around a rainbow array of vegetables. Raw or roasted, stewed or spiralised, grilled or grated, vegetables can be enjoyed in endless ways and here are some of my absolute favourite recipes for easy, stress-free lunches and dinners.'

I've recreated some of the most popular takeaways and street-food feasts, such as Pizza (p. 153) and Pad Thai Noodles (p. 136). And for the ultimate in comfort food, do try the lentil cottage pie with a golden cauliflower mash topping (p. 148). The Mexican Bean Burgers (p. 149) are seriously tasty too, not to mention the hearty vegetarian take on a French classic, boeuf bourguignon, starring mushrooms instead of beef and served alongside a creamy Butternut Mash (p. 156) – all in 30 minutes.

One of the simplest dishes to prepare, a real crowd-pleaser that will also use up all the leftover bits and pieces in your fridge, is the Chinese Fried Quinoa with Spicy Garlic Sesame Oil (p. 140). It uses up leftover quinoa (though you could use buckwheat or noodles instead) and takes just 10 minutes, all cooked in one pan. It tastes and feels like a takeaway (but better!) and is packed with flavour. It's also wholesome and, veg-wise, anything goes. The Thai Green Vegetable Curry on p. 143 is another lovely dish – full of spices and herbs. Make the curry paste in industrial quantities to store in the freezer so that you can whip up a curry whenever you like, without having to start from scratch each time.

During the working week, forget about making a special lunch each day and instead base it around dinner the night before. Three really great dinners that would double up as packed lunches without fear of getting soggy are the Spiced Halloumi & Chickpeas with Black Quinoa Tabbouleh (p. 150), the Warm Celeriac Salade Niçoise (p. 145) and the Broccoli Falafels with Tahini Lemon Drizzel (p. 146). And don't think twice about cooking in batches too. Whether that be making twice the batch of noodles, doubling up a dressing to use in a salad later in the week or roasting a few trays of vegetables, those few extra minutes spent now will mean you've got great components ready to go in the fridge all week.

For other vegetable mains try:

Lentil & Bean Chilli with Guacamole
  Bowl Food (p. 53)

Malaysian Coconut Noodle Soup
  Bowl Food (p. 68)

Monday Miso Noodle Soup
  Bowl Food (p. 46)

Tagine-style Stew
  Bowl Food (p. 54)

Mixing and matching other recipes

If you're vegetarian, do still have a look at the Fish and Meat chapters and take
inspiration from the vegetables there, such as the Herby Cauliflower Couscous (p. 125)
or Greek Salad (p. 117). Look at 'Sides' and 'Salads' too and see below for a few ideas
about how to pair up dishes to make a complete meal.

Carrot Fritters -
Sides (p. 200) with Za'atar Salad - Salads (p. 168)

Roast Vegetable Tray Bake -
Sides (p. 204) with Lentil Salad with Garlic Yoghurt Dressing -
Salads (p. 183)

Miso Veg Tray Bake -
Fish (p. 126) and Broccoli Rice - Basics (p. 272)

Spiced Beans and Halloumi -
Breakfast & Brunch (p. 35) and Quinoa Toast -Breakfast & Brunch (p. 21)

Tamarind Ginger Greens -
Fish (p. 131) and Coriander & Lime Quinoa - Sides (p. 192)

Pad Thai noodles

One of the most popular takeaways, pad Thai is easy to make at home and is a great way to use up leftover veg. The sweet, tangy sauce will convince many a reluctant veg eater to eat lots without hesitation. You can use any cabbage here and swap the buckwheat noodles with noodles of your choice. Tamarind paste is stocked in a variety of places, especially Asian shops. Don't skip the toasted peanuts and fresh herbs!

Serves 4

330g buckwheat noodles
6 spring onions, sliced (green parts saved to garnish)
4 garlic cloves, finely chopped
Extra-virgin olive oil
1 large pepper
2 large courgettes
½ cabbage (about 350g)
1½ tablespoons coconut oil
4 eggs
Sea salt and black pepper

PAD THAI SAUCE
4 tablespoons tamarind paste (or to taste)
4 tablespoons fish sauce
3½ tablespoons maple syrup
3 tablespoons tamari
Juice of 1 lime
1 teaspoon chilli flakes (or to taste)

TO SERVE
1 handful of peanuts or cashews
1 lime, cut into 4 wedges
1 handful of fresh coriander or Thai basil leaves, roughly chopped
Chilli flakes

1. Cook the noodles in a large pot of boiling water according to the packet instructions until al dente (about 5 minutes rather than the usual 6–8). Drain and then rinse in cold water before setting aside. Drizzle in a little olive oil to prevent them from sticking.

2. While the noodles are cooking, prepare the vegetables by either spiralizing them (p. 273) or peeling them into strips using a julienne or standard vegetable peeler.

3. Wipe the pot dry and place back on a medium heat, then add half the coconut oil and, when it has melted, crack in the eggs. Roughly scramble to break the yolks and allow to set for 30 seconds, then season with salt and pepper and flip one half over, like an omelette. Use your spoon or spatula to break into chunks and then tip onto a plate and set aside.

4. Melt the remaining coconut oil, add the spring onions and garlic and stir-fry for 1 minute, then turn up the heat, tip in the pepper and courgette strips and fry for 2 minutes. Stir in the cabbage and cook for a further 1 minute until the vegetables are tender but still with some bite.

5. Meanwhile, to make the Pad Thai sauce, whisk all of the sauce ingredients together. Add the sauce to the pan, turn up the heat and then add the noodles and toss everything together for a minute until well mixed (add a splash of water if it needs it) and turn off the heat.

6. Taste again for seasoning, adding a splash of tamari or salt if needed, then mix through the omelette chunks and serve up, letting everyone help themselves to nuts, lime wedges, spring onions, fresh herbs and chilli flakes.

✳ Use It Up

Swap the courgettes for 2 large carrots and use any nuts or seeds you have. For a meaty version of this dish, try prawns, flaked fish or shredded cooked chicken.

Spicy nutty noodles with fried eggs

Creamy, spicy, nutty noodles paired with just-cooked cabbage and a yolky egg . You'll always find cabbage and eggs in my fridge – they're two of my favourite ingredients, not to mention cheap! Use your choice of nut butter (smooth rather than chunky works best here), your choice of noodles and any type of cabbage – such as Savoy, pointed cabbage or spring greens. To cut through the richness of the sauce, try with a spoonful of kimchi or Quickly Pickled Veg (p. 199).

Serves 2

165g buckwheat noodles
Extra-virgin olive oil
2 tablespoons sesame seeds
2 teaspoons coconut oil
   or ghee
½ cabbage (500g),
   leaves finely shredded
3 spring onions, sliced
2 eggs
Sea salt and black pepper

SAUCE

2 garlic cloves, finely chopped
3 tablespoons peanut butter or
   other nut/seed butter (p. 276)
1-2 teaspoons chilli flakes or
   Korean chilli powder, plus
   extra to serve (or to taste)
1 tablespoon apple cider
   vinegar
2 teaspoons maple syrup
1 teaspoon toasted sesame oil
2 tablespoons tamari
3 tablespoons hot water
A pinch of sea salt (or to taste)

1. In a medium saucepan, cook the noodles in plenty of boiling water according to the packet instructions until still al dente (for about 5 minutes instead of the usual 6–8), then rinse in cold water and drain well. Drizzle in a little olive oil to prevent them from sticking.

2. Meanwhile, whisk all the sauce ingredients together and taste for seasoning.

3. In a large frying pan, toast the sesame seeds on a medium heat for 30 seconds, then set aside. Put the pan back on the hob, add the oil and quickly fry the shredded cabbage and spring onions on a high heat for 45 seconds (not too long, so the cabbage retains some bite). Push the cabbage to one side of the pan and fry the eggs, sunny side up, in the space. Season the eggs and cabbage with salt and pepper.

4. Rinse out the saucepan and put it back on the hob over a medium heat. Pour the sauce into the pan and heat through for 30 seconds, gently stir in the noodles to heat through and then remove from the hob.

5. Divide the hot noodles between two bowls, add a portion of cabbage and a fried egg to each bowl and sprinkle with chilli and the toasted sesame seeds, to serve.

Singapore noodles

The crunchy texture and gently spiced flavour of this dish are a sure-fire way of coaxing any veg-shy friends or family members to eat a wider range of vegetables. Feel free to change up the veg, too. As a rough guide, you want about 200g per person. You could also add an egg, like the one in Pad Thai Noodles (p. 136), and stir it through at the end.

Serves 4

330g buckwheat noodles
Extra-virgin olive oil
1 tablespoon coconut oil
6 spring onions, sliced
  (some green parts saved
  to garnish)
3 garlic cloves, chopped
3cm piece of ginger, finely
  chopped
1 teaspoon chilli flakes
  (or to taste)
1 handful of fresh coriander,
  stalks finely chopped and
  leaves roughly torn
500g mixed mushrooms
  (such as shiitake and
  chestnut), sliced
1 heaped tablespoon curry
  powder (or to taste)
1 large red pepper, deseeded
  and cut into strips
300g green beans, trimmed
  and chopped in half
300g mangetout
1 lime, halved
2 tablespoons tamari
1 tablespoon fish sauce
3 tablespoons hot water
Sea salt and black pepper

1. In a wide, deep pan cook the noodles in plenty of boiling water according to the packet instructions until al dente (about 5 minutes rather than the usual 6–8). Drain and then rinse in cold water and set aside. Drizzle in a little olive oil to prevent them from sticking.

2. Wipe out the pan and add the coconut oil. When the oil has melted, add most of the spring onions (reserving the green tops to serve) with the garlic, ginger, chilli and coriander stalks and fry over a medium heat for 2 minutes. Add the mushrooms and fry for 4 minutes, stirring occasionally, until any liquid released has been cooked off.

3. Turn up the heat, add most of the curry powder and all the veg, then stir-fry on a high heat for 5 minutes until the vegetables are just tender but still with bite.

4. Meanwhile, place the rest of the curry powder in a small bowl, squeeze in the juice of half a lime and mix with the tamari, fish sauce and hot water.

5. Once the vegetables are just tender, add the cooked noodles and the bowl of sauce and mix together to heat through. (You may find it easier to stir in half the noodles first, then add the rest and stir again.)

6. Remove from the heat and taste for seasoning, adding more curry powder to taste, then divide among bowls and top with the coriander leaves and the remaining lime half, cut into wedges.

✳ Use It Up

Try swapping the kale for any chopped leafy greens and the mangetout for sugar snap peas or small broccoli florets. Substitute the buckwheat noodles with any other kind of noodles or even Vegetable Noodles (p. 273).

Chinese fried quinoa with spicy garlic sesame oil

This is a veggie-packed, 15-minute home version of a Chinese takeaway. I have to eat it with chopsticks to make myself slow down – it's that good! It's an ideal way to use up leftover quinoa and you just need 10 minutes to chop everything up so that it's ready to go, then simply fry it all together, serve up and make a super-speedy spicy garlic sesame oil to go on top. Top with a fried yolky egg or scramble in a few eggs, as in Thai Cauliflower Rice (p. 112), and serve with some kimchi on the side.

Serves 4

1 tablespoon coconut oil
6 spring onions, sliced
(green parts saved to
garnish)
1 teaspoon chilli flakes
(or to taste)
3 garlic cloves, finely chopped
1 large carrot, finely chopped
200g green beans, trimmed
and finely sliced
2 large courgettes,
finely chopped
1 large red pepper, deseeded
and diced
1 quantity of cooked quinoa
(p. 150)
2 tablespoons tamari
Sea salt and black pepper

GARLIC SESAME OIL
1 tablespoon coconut oil
2 garlic cloves, finely chopped
1 teaspoon chilli flakes
(or to taste)
1 tablespoon tamari
1 tablespoon toasted sesame
oil
½ teaspoon Chinese five-spice
powder

1. In a large, wide frying pan, melt the oil over a medium-high heat and fry the white parts of the spring onions with the chilli flakes and garlic for 1 minute, stirring occasionally so they soften but don't brown.

2. Add the carrot and green beans and cook for 1 minute, then add the courgettes and red pepper and stir-fry for another minute.

3. Stir in the cooked quinoa and the tamari, turn the heat up to high and cook for 2 minutes until the quinoa is heathed through and until it's a little crispy on the bottom.

4. Divide among bowls and top with the leftover green parts of the spring onions.

5. Straight away, put the pan back on a low heat, add the oil and when the oil has melted, stir-fry the garlic for 30 seconds to soften but not brown. Take off the heat, add the chilli flakes, tamari, toasted sesame oil and five-spice powder, then tip the mix into a little bowl and let everyone help themselves. A little goes a long way!

 Use It Up

You can really fridge-and-freezer forage here to use up any veg that needs eating.

● Tip

Don't worry too much about perfect dicing. The vegetables just need to be chopped to roughly the same size so that they cook evenly.

Thai green vegetable curry

One of my all-time favourite curries, this is a really simple version that still hits the spot and takes less time than ordering a takeaway. To keep things easier, this uses ginger instead of galangal and lime zest instead of kaffir lime leaves. Triple or quadruple this paste and divide into portions to keep in the freezer, so you've got your own paste ready to go whenever you want. I like to cook the vegetables so they are just tender, and you can adapt the dish to include chicken, prawns or fish. Oh, and remember to get green chillies if you want this to look green – otherwise it will be a red curry! Serve with Buckwheat Naans for an Indian twist (p. 191) or Chickpea Wraps (p. 190) as pictured here.

Serves 4

1 x 400ml tin of coconut milk
150ml stock (p. 278) or water
1 aubergine, cut into
    1.5cm chunks
2 courgettes, cut into
    1.5cm chunks
16 cherry tomatoes, halved
300g green beans, trimmed
    and halved
1 tablespoon tamari
1 tablespoon fish sauce
Thai Basil leaves, to serve
Lime wedges, to serve

CURRY PASTE
4 garlic cloves, peeled
1 large onion, quartered
Stalks of 2 handfuls of fresh
    coriander (leaves saved to
    garnish)
Stalks of 1 large handful of
    basil (leaves saved to
    garnish)
1–2 green chillies, deseeded
3cm piece of ginger
2 lemongrass stalks (tough
    outer leaves removed),
    roughly chopped
1 teaspoon ground coriander
1 teaspoon ground cumin
Juice and grated zest of 1 lime
A big pinch of sea salt

1. Place all the ingredients for the curry paste in a food processor and blend until smooth.

2. Heat up a wide, deep pan and fry the paste over a low-medium heat for about 5 minutes, stirring occasionally until the raw ingredients no longer smell as pungent. If the paste gets too dry, add a splash of water so it doesn't burn.

3. Add the coconut milk, stock, aubergine and courgettes. Bring to a medium simmer and cook for 6 minutes with a lid on the pan.

4. Tip in the tomatoes and beans and cook for a further 5 minutes until the beans are tender. Add the tamari and fish sauce and taste for seasoning: you might want to add more tamari or salt or a little extra lime juice. Scatter with basil leaves and the leftover coriander leaves, and serve with the lime wedges.

✳ Use It Up

Swap the courgettes for carrots or squash (which will need longer to cook), and the green beans for mangetout, sugar snap peas or broccoli florets.

● Tip

If you're unsure of how strong you like your chilli, start with just one. You can always chop up another chilli and add it later when you've tasted the curry.

Turkish wraps with spinach & feta

I celebrated my 30th birthday in Istanbul and this reminds me of the street food there – some of the best in the world. The quick Chickpea Wraps (p. 190) are perfect with this, or pile onto a buckwheat pizza base (p. 153) to make a Turkish-style pizza, but you could also serve the spinach and feta mixture with other sides, such as cooked quinoa, beans or lentils. These would go well with a fresh salad or simple slaw on the side, such as the chopped salad on p. 94.

Serves 2

2 teaspoons butter or ghee
1 onion, finely chopped
1 large red pepper, deseeded
   and sliced into strips
2 garlic cloves, finely chopped
2 teaspoons dried oregano or
   thyme
300g spinach
150g feta, crumbled
Juice of ½ lemon
1 small handful of fresh mint
   leaves, roughly chopped
2 tablespoons of extra-virgin
   olive oil
Sea salt and black pepper

TO SERVE
1 teaspoon chilli flakes, ideally
   Aleppo pepper (pul biber)
1 small handful of sesame
   seeds
4 medium Chickpea Wraps
   (p. 190 – made plain, with no
   additions, and warmed
   through if you like)

1. Make the wraps (p. 190), or if you have some ready to go then put them in a low oven to warm through. Heat a wide pan and add the butter. When the butter has melted, add the onion and fry for 3 minutes, then add the red pepper, garlic and dried herbs and fry for another 2 minutes, stirring occasionally.

2. Turn up the heat, stir in the spinach and cook for another 1–2 minutes, with a lid on the pan, until the spinach has wilted.

3. Remove from the heat, then stir through half the feta, add the lemon juice and extra-virgin olive oil, and season with black pepper. Stir in the mint and taste for seasoning; the feta will be salty, so you may only need to add a small pinch of salt.

4. Sprinkle over the remaining feta, along with the chilli flakes and seeds and put the pan on the table, with a pile of chickpea wraps to assemble as you eat.

 Use It Up

Swap the spinach for chard or other leafy greens and cook for 3 minutes in step 2. Replace the mint with dill or parsley.

● Tip

If you get time brush the wraps with oil, fold in half and cook until golden and crisp.

Warm celeriac salade niçoise

This is one of my favourite lunchbox-friendly salads, featuring a fabulous French dressing. Here I use celeriac instead of the traditional waxy potatoes. I keep a few small jars of olives, sun-dried tomatoes and capers in the fridge. They're expensive but a little goes a long way, turning a meal like this into something very special.

Serves 4

400ml boiling water
1 large celeriac (about 800g), peeled and cut into 1.5cm cubes
350g green beans, trimmed
6 eggs
1 handful of pitted olives or 2 tablespoons capers
1 handful of sun-dried tomatoes, chopped, or cherry tomatoes, halved
1 handful of fresh herbs (such as basil or parsley), chopped
300g lettuce (such as Little Gem or butter lettuce), leaves separated and torn
Sea salt and black pepper

FRENCH DRESSING
6 tablespoons extra-virgin olive oil
2 tablespoons apple cider vinegar
2 teaspoons mustard (or to taste)
1 garlic clove, finely chopped
1 shallot or ½ small onion, finely chopped
1 teaspoon raw honey or maple syrup (optional)

1. Pour boiling water into a saucepan on a medium heat and add a big pinch of salt. Drop in the celeriac pieces to simmer for 3 minutes, then add the green beans and cook for a further 6 minutes until the vegetables are tender. Remove from the heat and drain well.

2. Meanwhile, whisk the dressing ingredients together in a large serving bowl and season to taste with salt and pepper. Add the drained vegetables and toss in the dressing while still warm to absorb the flavours.

3. Fill the pan again with boiling water, lower in the eggs and boil for 6½ minutes until soft-boiled, then drain and leave in a bowl of cold or iced water for 5 minutes. Peel the eggs as soon as they are cool enough to handle, then blot dry with kitchen paper.

4. Meanwhile, place all the other salad ingredients in the serving bowl and toss gently to coat in the dressing. Cut the eggs in half, sprinkle with salt and pepper and arrange on top of the salad. Serve warm or pack up for a working lunch (see tip).

✳ Use It Up

You could swap the celeriac for cubes of roast butternut squash or beetroot, for a beautiful contrast in colour, or add flaked fish, tinned anchovies or smoked mackerel, if you like.

 Tip

If packing for lunch, lay the salad leaves on top, so they don't get crushed, and keep the eggs whole.

Broccoli falafels with tahini lemon drizzle

I adore falafels but have had too many dry ones for my liking. These are made with broccoli, along with the more traditional chickpeas, which sneaks in more veg and keeps them moist. Serve in lettuce leaves or Chickpea Wraps (p. 190) with Quickly Pickled Veg (p. 199) or some shredded raw vegetables like carrots and onions. They would also be delicious as part of a packed lunch. Try them with cauliflower, too, and make extra tahini lemon drizzle to dress salads or spoon over leftover roasted veg.

Makes 30 small falafels

½ head of broccoli (150g), chopped into florets
½ onion, roughly chopped
2 garlic cloves, peeled
1 large handful of mixed fresh herbs (such as parsley and mint)
1 x 400g tin of chickpeas, drained and rinsed
Grated zest of ½ lemon
2 teaspoons ground cumin
1 teaspoon ground coriander
¼ teaspoon cayenne pepper
3 tablespoons flour (such as buckwheat or chickpea)
1 teaspoon baking powder
Sea salt and black pepper

TAHINI DRIZZLE
8 tablespoons tahini
Juice of 1 lemon
250ml warm water
2 garlic cloves, finely chopped
Sea salt and black pepper

1. Preheat the oven to fan 220°C/Gas mark 9 and line two baking trays with baking parchment.

2. Using a food processor, blitz the broccoli, pulsing for 10 seconds each time, until it resembles 'rice'. Remove and repeat with the onion, garlic and herbs. Return the broccoli 'rice' to the food processor.

3. Add all the remaining ingredients for the falafels and 1 teaspoon of salt. Pulse until combined, rather than blitzing until smooth, so that some chickpea chunks remain. (This takes about a minute – you may need to scrape down the sides of the food processor.) Taste for seasoning, adding pepper and more salt, if you like.

4. Using damp hands, pinch off 30 pieces of the mixture (just under 1 tablespoon each) and roll them into balls. Place on the lined trays and bake in the oven for 18 minutes, turning halfway through. Then remove the trays from the oven, turn the balls over and let them bake for a further 4 minutes.

5. Meanwhile, make the tahini drizzle by whisking all the ingredients together. Place on the table with the falafels and let everyone help themselves. Serve with the chickpea wraps (p.190), as pictured here, or with lettuce or cabbage cups.

✳ Use It Up

If you have some lettuce leaves that need eating up, shape the falafel mixture into eight burgers instead and bake them in the oven for 25 minutes, serving with the lettuce leaves as a burger bun.

Mexican bean burgers

These are seriously good bean burgers that hit the spot in every way. Crisp and moist, spiced and salty, they are quick to make and really satisfying. Top with Guacamole (p. 53) and serve in cabbage cups or lettuce wraps or with Coriander & Lime Quinoa (p. 192). These burgers freeze well uncooked, so why not make a double batch and freeze half. You could also shape the mixture into bean balls, instead of burgers, and serve them with a bowl of guacamole or Garlic Yoghurt (p.183) to dip in as a starter or snack.

Serves 4

1½ tablespoons coconut oil
   or ghee
1 onion, finely chopped
2 garlic cloves, finely chopped
1 large handful of fresh
   coriander, leaves and stalks
   finely chopped
1 tablespoon tomato purée
2 teaspoons ground cumin
1 teaspoon chilli
   flakes (or to taste)
2 x 400g tins of white beans
   (such as cannellini, butter
   beans or chickpeas)
Juice and grated zest of 1 lime
4–5 tablespoons flour (such
   as buckwheat or chickpea) or
   ground almonds
   or ground almonds
Sea salt and black pepper

1. Melt ½ tablespoon of oil in a wide frying pan. Add the onion and fry on a medium heat for 6 minutes until softened, stirring from time to time.

2. Add the garlic, coriander stalks, tomato purée, spices and chilli and cook for 2 minutes, stirring occasionally to prevent them from burning.

3. Meanwhile, place the beans in a bowl with the lime juice and zest and mash with a fork, so that some of the beans are well mashed and some are kept whole. Add the flour, coriander leaves, the fried onion and spice mixture. Mix together well and season to taste. If the mixture is a bit wet, add a little more flour.

4. Divide the bean mixture into quarters and, using damp hands, mould each quarter into a burger about 2cm thick and 8cm wide.

5. Heat the same pan up, melt the remaining oil and fry the burgers over a medium-high heat for 4 minutes, on each side, until nicely browned.

 Tip

Use dried or fresh chilli, and look out for chipotle and jalapeño too.

Veggie cottage pie with cauliflower mash

This cottage pie is jam-packed with tasty veg and lentils and topped with a comforting cauliflower cheese mash. To save on washing up, use an ovenproof pan to cook the filling so that the whole pie can go straight from the hob to the grill for the mash topping to get golden. I recommend doubling the recipe: make one to eat straight away and one to pop in the freezer (before you grill the top). Defrost the second pie when needed, and heat through in the oven at fan 190°C/Gas mark 6½ for 25 minutes or until browned on top.

Serves 4

1 tablespoon butter or ghee
1 large onion, finely chopped
3 garlic cloves, finely chopped
1½ teaspoons dried rosemary
   or thyme
1 large handful of fresh
   parsley, stalks and leaves
   finely chopped
2 carrots, finely chopped
2 courgettes, finely chopped
1 tablespoon tomato purée
1 x 400ml tin of chopped
   tomatoes
200ml stock (p. 278) or water
2 x 400g tins of lentils (Puy,
   green or brown), drained
   and rinsed
2 large handfuls of frozen peas
Sea salt and black pepper

CAULIFLOWER MASH
2 cauliflowers (total 800g),
   chopped into equal-sized
   florets
160ml water
1 tablespoon butter, plus extra
   to serve
1 large handful of grated
   cheese (such as mature
   Cheddar or Parmesan)

1. In a wide, large ovenproof pan, melt the butter, then add the onion and fry over a medium heat for 4 minutes, stirring halfway through.

2. Add the garlic, dried herbs and parsley stalks, followed by the carrots and courgettes, and cook for another 5 minutes, stirring from time to time.

3. Add the tomato purée, tinned tomatoes and stock. Season with salt and pepper, then bring to a simmer on a medium-high heat and cook for 8 minutes until the sauce has thickened and reduced.

4. Meanwhile, make the mash. Place the cauliflower in a separate pan and pour in the water. Cover with a lid, then turn the heat up to medium-high and steam for 5 minutes until tender. Drain the water from the pan and return the florets to the dry pan, then add the butter and roughly mash with a potato masher, seasoning with salt and pepper to taste.

5. Preheat the grill to high. Add the lentils to the vegetable pan and simmer on a medium heat for another 3 minutes, then taste for seasoning and stir in the parsley leaves and frozen peas to heat through for a final minute. The filling should be relatively thick but with a good gravy – add a splash of water if it's getting dry.

6. Make sure the pie filling is even and level in the pan, then spoon over the cauliflower mash and add either a handful of grated cheese on top or dot with more butter. Score the top with the back of a fork and grill for 5 minutes until golden brown.

✳ Use It Up

Any leftover veg goes well here - the last few stalks of celery or a bit of squash and sweet potato.

Spiced halloumi & chickpeas with black quinoa tabbouleh

A one-pan dish packed with crunch, freshness and spice. Quinoa is protein-rich and the black version, if you can get it, looks beautiful set against the herbs and salad leaves. Regular quinoa is just as good – but it needs 2 minutes less cooking time – or you could use red quinoa instead and cook for the same length of time as the black quinoa. The combination of spiced salty-sweet fried halloumi and chickpeas is unbeatable – you'll be wanting to use this pairing with everything. This makes a bit extra and any leftovers make a great packed lunch.

Serves 2

1 tablespoon coconut oil
1 teaspoon ground cumin
1 teaspoon smoked paprika
1 teaspoon chilli flakes
1 x 400g tin of chickpeas, drained and rinsed
250g halloumi, chopped into 2cm cubes
2 teaspoons maple syrup

TABBOULEH
500ml water or stock (p. 278)
200g black quinoa, rinsed well
3 tomatoes, finely chopped
½ cucumber, diced
1 small red onion, finely chopped
Juice and zest of 1 lemon
6 tablespoons extra-virgin olive oil
3 large handfuls of salad leaves (watercress or rocket)
4 large handfuls of fresh parsley, stalks and leaves finely chopped
1 large handful of fresh mint leaves, roughly chopped
Sea salt and black pepper

TO SERVE
1 small handful of pistachios or other nuts
1 small handful of pomegranate seeds or dried fruit

1. First make the quinoa for the tabbouleh. Pour the water or stock into a large, wide pan, cover with a lid and bring to the boil. Add the quinoa and bring back up to the boil, then reduce the heat to medium, cover and simmer for about 17 minutes until all the liquid has been absorbed and the quinoa is tender. (If the quinoa has been soaked first, simmer for 15 minutes). Uncover, fluff the quinoa with a fork and set aside to allow to cool.

2. Meanwhile, place all the other tabbouleh ingredients except for the leaves and herbs in a large serving bowl and mix together.

3. Tip the cooked quinoa into the serving bowl, mix everything together. The quinoa will soak up the flavours as it starts to cool.

4. Wipe the pan dry, then melt the oil, add the spices and stir for a minute over a medium heat.

5. Turn up the heat, add the chickpeas and halloumi, tossing in the spicy oil, and fry for 45 seconds until golden brown. Toss again and fry the halloumi on the other side for another 30 seconds. Drizzle over the maple syrup, add a pinch of salt and leave to bubble for 30 seconds. Toss once more to coat in the salty-sweet oil.

6. Mix the tabbouleh with the salad leaves and herbs and then add the halloumi and chickpeas. Serve scattered with pistachios or other nuts, pomegranate seeds or dried fruit, if you like.

Buckwheat pizza

The buckwheat dough used for this pizza base is really easy to knock up and is so versatile. (It's the same type of dough used on p. 191 to make Buckwheat Naans.) It's delicious covered in this very simple tomato sauce with cheese scattered on top, but feel free to go crazy with any toppings of your choice. In addition to the ideas suggested below, you could add roasted peppers or artichoke hearts from a jar, or add an egg to a layer of just wilted garlic spinach for a Florentine-style pizza.

Makes 8 small pizzas

1 quantity of Buckwheat Naan
    dough (p. 191), plus extra
    buckwheat flour for dusting
200g Parmesan or mozzarella

TOMATO SAUCE
1 tablespoon butter or ghee
2 garlic cloves, finely chopped
1 tablespoon tomato purée
1 x 400g tin of chopped
    tomatoes or 400ml passata
1½ teaspoons dried oregano
Sea salt and black pepper

TO SERVE
200g rocket
1 handful of fresh basil leaves,
    torn
Extra-virgin olive oil, for
    drizzling

1. Preheat the oven to fan 220°C/Gas mark 9 and line two to three large baking trays with baking parchment.

2. Melt the butter in a medium pan, add the garlic and fry over a medium heat for 30 seconds until softened, then stir through the tomato purée and cook for another 30 seconds. Add the chopped tomatoes and oregano and bring to the boil. Reduce the heat to medium and simmer, half covered, for 15 minutes to reduce to a thick sauce, stirring halfway through.

3. Roll the buckwheat dough into a sausage about 4cm wide and divide into eight pieces. Sprinkle some buckwheat flour onto each of the lined trays, dust your fingers with flour and spread and flatten each piece of dough into a circle 8–10 cm in diameter and 4mm thick (being careful not to tear the dough). Place the dough circles on the baking trays, allowing about three per tray and 2–3cm between each circle.

4. Season to taste, then spread a little of the tomato sauce (just under 1 tablespoon) onto each base, making sure you don't use too much as the pizza will become soggy.

5. Add any optional extras, then grate over some Parmesan, or dot around a few chunks of mozzarella, and bake in the oven for 8–10 minutes until the cheese is melted and golden and the base is crispy. Serve with fresh rocket and basil leaves, either scattered on top or piled on the side, and a little drizzle of olive oil.

✳ Use It Up

Leftover broccoli and other greens make a great pizza topping, or add a few thinly sliced mushrooms and courgettes as pictured here.

Squash 'rice' Spanish-style

I've swapped the main ingredient, rice, for squash in this paella-esque dish. Butternut squash is turned into small rice-sized pieces and fried with lots of garlic, vegetables and Spanish flavourings. You could also make this with quinoa or cauliflower rice – I say anything goes! For how to make Vegetable Rice, see p. 272. Serve straight from the pan topped with some simple Garlic Yoghurt (p. 183).

Serves 4

2 tablespoons coconut oil
  or ghee
1 x 400g tin of chickpeas,
  rinsed and drained
1 large red onion, finely
  chopped
2 peppers, deseeded and sliced
  into thin strips
200g green beans, trimmed
3 garlic cloves, finely chopped
¼ teaspoon cayenne pepper
1 teaspoon smoked paprika
100ml stock (p. 278) or water
2 tablespoons apple cider
  vinegar
1 x 400g tin of chopped
  tomatoes
1 teaspoon saffron threads,
  soaked in a few tablespoons
  of warm water (optional)
1 butternut squash (about
  1kg), peeled, deseeded and
  grated into 'rice' (p. 272)
200g frozen peas
1 tablespoon lemon juice
Sea salt and black pepper

TO SERVE
1 handful of antipasto-style
  artichoke hearts, quartered
1 handful of pitted olives,
  halved
1 large handful of fresh
  parsley leaves, chopped
1 large lemon, sliced into
  wedges
Garlic Yoghurt (p. 183)

1. In a very large, wide pan, melt half of the oil and add the drained chickpeas to the pan. Fry on a high heat, tossing occasionally, until golden and slightly crunchy (about 4 minutes). Season to taste then set aside.

2. Melt the remaining half of the oil in the same pan, then add the onion and fry over a medium-high heat for 4 minutes until starting to soften. Add the peppers, green beans, garlic, cayenne pepper and paprika and cook for 3 minutes, stirring occasionally. Add a little of the stock or water if the mixture is starting to stick.

3. Add the apple cider vinegar and let it reduce for a minute on a high heat, then add the tomatoes, stock, saffron and its soaking liquid (if using). Turn up the heat, add the squash rice and cook for 6-8 minutes, stirring from time to time, until there is no visible liquid and the squash is tender with a little bite (liked cooked rice). Stir in the peas and cook for a final 2 minutes, then turn off the heat, stir through the lemon juice and taste for seasoning.

4. Tuck in the artichoke hearts and the olives, then sprinkle over the parsley. Scatter with the crunchy chickpeas, add a dollop of garlic yoghurt and serve with lemon wedges.

❋ Use It Up

Swap with whatever vegetables you have to hand – it would be equally delicious with fennel, aubergines, asparagus, mushrooms and broad beans.

You can substitute the chickpeas with any other kind of tinned bean, or use two handfuls of cooked quinoa.

Mushroom bourguignon with butternut mash

A bourguignon is traditionally made with beef and simmered for hours; this mushroom version has all the rich flavour of the French classic while being tailor-made for a busy evening. It goes beautifully with Butternut Squash Mash (p.156) and Broccoli & Beans (p.203) as pictured here, though for a quicker side you could serve with Cauliflower Mash (p. 274) instead. I like to make extra mash for enjoying later in the week but if you'd prefer to not cook up a side, serve this with some leftover quinoa, a big side salad, or enjoy it as it comes.

Serves 4

2 tablespoons butter or ghee
1 large red onion, finely
   chopped
4 garlic cloves, finely chopped
2 celery sticks, diced
2 large carrots, diced
1 tablespoon chopped fresh
   thyme or rosemary leaves
1 large handful of fresh
   parsley, stalks finely chopped
   and leaves roughly chopped
3 tablespoons tomato purée
750g mushrooms (such as
   portobello or wild), roughly
   chopped
1 large glass of red wine
   (250ml)
400ml stock (p. 278) or water
1 x 400ml tin of lentils (Puy,
   brown or green), drained
   and rinsed
Sea salt and black pepper

BUTTERNUT MASH
1 butternut squash (800g),
   peeled, deseeded and
   chopped into 2cm chunks
200ml boiling water
1 garlic clove, roughly chopped
1 tablespoon butter

1. In a large, deep saucepan, melt the butter, add the onion and fry on a medium heat for 4 minutes until softened, stirring occasionally.

2. Add the garlic, celery, carrots, thyme and parsley stalks and cook for 4 minutes, stirring from time to time. Add the tomato purée and cook for another 1 minute.

3. Turn the heat up to high, tip in the mushrooms (which will fill the pan) and the wine. Give the mixture a good stir and let the wine bubble off for a couple of minutes.

4. Pour in the stock or water and bring to a medium simmer, put a lid on the pan and cook for 10 minutes, then stir in the lentils and cook for another 4 minutes, uncovered, for the sauce to thicken and reduce. (See tip.)

5. Meanwhile, place the butternut squash in a wide, deep pan, add the boiling water and the garlic, then cover with a lid and steam for 12–14 minutes until tender. Drain well and return to the pan, then add the butter and mash, either by hand using a potato masher or in a food processor, and season to taste.

6. Taste the mushroom bourguignon for seasoning, stir in the chopped parsley leaves and serve with the mash.

 Tip

For an extra-thick sauce, blitz one corner of the bourguignon pan contents with a hand-held blender for a few seconds, if you like, and then stir into the rest of the stew.

SALADS

'THIS chapter is bursting with delicious and speedy salads to enjoy all year round. A salad can really take any shape you want: cold and crunchy, warm with some cooked lentils soaking up a dressing (p. 183) or with hot elements like bacon and asparagus (p. 180). Salads can be small, to eat as a starter or a side, or used as a base to build into a satisfying main. '

Mostly I like my salads to have big flavours, a riot of colours and tonnes of texture. If I'm having people over, I don't plate up individual starters; I'll make up a huge platter of one of these salads and let everyone help themselves. The Salsa Salad (p. 176) would work well for a group or try the wonderfully colourful and refreshing Watermelon, Feta & Griddled Avocado Salad on p. 162.

A few of these dishes use expensive items like buffalo mozzarella or figs, which I save for special occasions and when they are in season, but most of the salads are based on affordable ingredients, such as carrots and cabbage – ideal for knocking up a quick slaw (p. 177). Slaws are especially handy because, like a kale salad (p. 174), they don't wilt and last a good few days in the fridge.

Quality seasonal ingredients and ripe produce need little more than vinegar and some extra-virgin olive oil to dress them, like the Caprese Salad with Figs (p. 172). But a great dressing takes most salads to the next level, and you can save time by making double or triple batches, keeping extra in a jar in the fridge. A couple of my favourite dressings for multipurpose use are the Olive Dressing (p. 162) and Avocado Dressing (p. 174), along with the Ginger Tahini Dressing (p. 166). It's mixed with cold noodles here, but this last dressing would be equally delicious over roasted aubergines or fried kale.

Any of the salads in this chapter could be adapted for a packed lunch. You can either store the dressing separately to prevent soggy leaves, or dress more 'robust' salads the night before, as they will still be great come lunchtime. This includes the Lentil Salad (p. 183), Freestyle Quinoa Salad (p. 165), Hot-smoked Trout with a Beetroot Fennel Salad (p. 178) and the Ginger Noodle Salad (p. 166).

You could also beef up these salads by serving with simple extras – hearty roast celeriac, squash or some cooked lentils and beans, leftover chicken or fish, quinoa or noodles. And mix and match these dishes with some of the side dishes in other chapters: the Spicy Thai Beef Salad (p. 182) with Cauliflower Rice (p. 272) or the Za'atar Salad (p. 168) with Roast Carrots with Pomegranate Molasses (p. 188).

For more salad ideas try:

Black Quinoa Tabbouleh
Vegetable Mains (p. 130)

Chopped Salad
Meat (p. 94)

Greek Salad
Fish (p. 117)

Herby Cauliflower Couscous
Fish (p. 125)

Pea & Rocket Salad
Fish (p. 116)

Quickly Pickled Veg
Sides (p. 199)

Cheeky Tzatziki
Snacks (p. 218)

Warm Celeriac Salade Niçoise
Vegetable Mains (p. 145)

Watermelon, feta & griddled avocado with olive dressing

A colourful and refreshing summer salad topped with feta and griddled avocado, this is a great way to feed a crowd. Make sure all your produce is ripe, so that the salad is full of flavour. This punchy, salty dressing keeps well in the fridge and is delicious on simple tomato salads or drizzled over fish, roast chicken or vegetables. If the weather's too hot to even think about switching on the hob, just slice up the avocado to serve.

Serves 4 as a side

Flesh of 1 large avocado,
   sliced into wedges
4 large tomatoes, roughly
   chopped
½ watermelon (about 500g),
   peeled and roughly chopped
200g feta, roughly crumbled
1 handful of fresh mint leaves,
   torn, to serve

OLIVE DRESSING
150g pitted olives
1 garlic clove, peeled
7 tablespoons extra-virgin
   olive oil
4 tablespoons apple cider
   vinegar
2 teaspoon raw honey or
   maple syrup
Sea salt and black pepper

1. Make the dressing by roughly blitzing all the ingredients together in a food processor or high-powered blender, seasoning with salt and pepper, to taste.

2. Set a griddle pan over a medium heat, add the avocado wedges and cook for 1½ minutes on each side, or until griddle marks appear.

3. Place the tomatoes and watermelon in a large serving bowl and top with the feta and griddled avocado wedges. Drizzle over half the dressing, scatter with the torn mint leaves and serve more dressing on the side.

Sesame carrot & courgette noodles salad/stir-fry

This dish is equally lovely as a salad or a stir-fry. The stir-fry is almost as quick to make as the salad, as it takes just an extra three minutes. When it comes to turning the carrots and courgettes into noodles, the larger they are the better, as smaller vegetables are more fiddly to work with. You can turn this into more of a main meal by doubling the quantity of dressing and combining with buckwheat noodles, cooked quinoa or with shredded chicken or fish. Store any leftover dressing in the fridge for spooning over roast aubergine or broccoli. And look out for yellow courgettes and purple carrots for a really special salad.

Serves 4 as a side

2 large carrots
2 large courgettes
4 spring onions, finely
   chopped
2 handfuls of mixed herbs
   (such as coriander, mint and
   Thai basil, roughly
   chopped
1 tablespoon coconut oil, for
   stir-frying only
1 handful of nuts or seeds
   (such as toasted peanuts
   or sesame seeds), to serve
   (optional)

DRESSING
1 fresh red chilli, deseeded and
   finely chopped (or to taste)
4 tablespoons extra-virgin
   olive oil
2 tablespoons toasted
   sesame oil
Juice of 1 lemon
1 teaspoon raw honey or
   maple syrup
1 tablespoon fish sauce or
   tamari
Sea salt and black pepper

1. In a large bowl, whisk all the dressing ingredients together, seasoning to taste with salt and pepper.

2. Turn the carrots and courgettes into noodles, either by spiralizing or using a julienne or standard vegetable peeler (p. 273).

3. **Salad:** Place the vegetable noodles in a large serving bowl and add the spring onions and fresh herbs. Toss in the dressing and scatter over the nuts or seeds (if using).

   Stir-fry: Melt the coconut oil in a wide frying pan, add the carrot noodles and stir-fry on a medium heat for 1 minute, then add the courgettes and stir-fry for 2 minutes. Stir in the dressing and heat through for 30 seconds, then remove from the heat and serve with the spring onions, herbs and nuts or seeds (if using).

Freestyle quinoa salad

Feeling confident about cooking freestyle is one of the best kitchen skills to acquire! You can then view recipes as more of a guide to play around with than a strict set of rules. This recipe is a good example of how to change things up, using cooked quinoa as a base and then combining it with a bit of crunch from nuts and seeds, chewy sweetness from dried fruits and freshness from the greens. Enjoy warm or cold. If you're making this in advance, don't add the green salad leaves until the end to ensure that they stay fresh and crisp.

Serves 6 as a side

500ml stock/bone broth
(p. 278) or water
200g white, red or black
quinoa, rinsed well (ideally
soaked first, p. 277)
1 tablespoon coconut oil
or ghee
1 large onion, thinly sliced
3 garlic cloves, finely chopped
Sea salt and black pepper

TAHINI DRESSING
6 tablespoons extra-virgin
olive oil
1 tablespoon tahini
Juice and grated zest of
1 lemon

1. Pour the stock into a wide saucepan, cover with a lid and bring to the boil. Add the quinoa, bring to a medium simmer and cook for about 15 minutes (or 13 minutes if the quinoa has been soaked first) until the quinoa is tender. (Red or black quinoa will take about 3 minutes longer).

2. Meanwhile, in a wide frying pan, dry-toast any nuts or seeds over a medium heat for 1 minute, shaking halfway through and taking care not to burn them, then set aside.

3. Place the pan back on a medium heat, melt the oil and fry the onion for 5 minutes until softened. Add the garlic and cook for a further minute.

4. Whisk all the dressing ingredients together in a large serving bowl and season to taste. Add the cooked quinoa, as well as the onion and garlic mixture and stir to combine.

5. Gently toss through your choice of nuts/seeds, dried fruits and fresh greens and any other ingredients.

OPTIONS FOR NUTS/SEEDS
AND DRIED FRUITS
1 large handful of nuts
(such as almonds, pistachios
or hazelnuts)
1 large handful of seeds
(such as sunflower, pumpkin
or pine nuts)
1 large handful of dried fruits
(such as goji berries,
cranberries or raisins)

OPTIONS FOR FRESH
GREENS
2 large handfuls of fresh herbs
(such as parsley, basil, mint
or dill), roughly chopped
200g salad leaves (such as
rocket, watercress or baby
spinach)
Flesh of 1 large ripe cubed
avocado or 1 finely sliced
fennel

Refreshing ginger noodle & seaweed salad

Inspired by the chilled Japanese-style soba noodle salad, this is a delicious way to eat seaweed. Any dried seaweed will do here – try arame, wakame or sea spaghetti, but if you can't find any, still make this. The creamy ginger tahini dressing would go well with some stir-fried kale or mushrooms. You don't need to chill the salad before eating, but it's so refreshing eaten straight from the fridge on a hot day to cool you down.

Serves 4

330g buckwheat noodles
Extra-virgin olive oil
2 tablespoons dried seaweed
(total 10g)
1 large cucumber
2 large peppers
150g radishes
6 spring onions, sliced

GINGER TAHINI DRESSING
3cm piece of ginger, grated
1 large garlic clove, finely
chopped
3 tablespoons tahini
Juice of ½ lemon
2 teaspoons raw honey or
maple syrup
1 tablespoon tamari
6 tablespoons water
Sea salt and black pepper

TO SERVE
2 tablespoons sesame seeds
1 large handful of fresh
coriander, roughly chopped

1. Cook the noodles in plenty of boiling water according to the packet instructions (6–8 minutes), then rinse in cold water and drain well before setting aside. Drizzle in a little oil to stop them sticking.

2. Meanwhile, soak the seaweed in a small bowl of water according to the packet instructions (about 8 minutes), then drain, rinse in fresh water and chop up or snip before setting aside.

3. In the meantime, make the dressing. Squeeze the grated ginger into a large serving bowl (it should yield about 2 teaspoons of ginger juice), add the remaining dressing ingredients and whisk together until smooth. Season to taste then add the soaked seaweed and cooked noodles to the bowl.

4. Make the cucumber and peppers into noodles by either spiralizing or using a julienne or standard vegetable peeler (p. 273). Scoop out the cucumber seeds if using a julienne/vegetable peeler. Add to a serving bowl with the radishes, spring onions and then toss everything together.

5. Put the bowl in the fridge to chill for 15 minutes (or until you're ready), then toss again and serve topped with sesame seeds and coriander.

Za'atar salad

Za'atar (meaning 'thyme') is a Middle Eastern dried herb mix that is wonderful in a variety of dishes, so do get your hands on some. It's normally made up of sesame seeds, sumac and thyme, with oregano or marjoram, and can be cooked with or used as a garnish. Try sprinkling it on dips, like the Roasted & Spiced Carrot Hummus (p. 213), or fried eggs. To build this salad into a main, serve with quinoa, lentils or roast vegetables or with the Spiced Lamb Chops (p. 98) and use red chicory, if you can get it, as it looks so beautiful.

Serves 4 as a side

2 heads of red chicory,
    roughly chopped
Leaves of 1 large lettuce, or
    4 Little Gem lettuces,
    roughly chopped or torn
1 cucumber, halved lengthways,
    deseeded (see tip) and sliced
    at an angle
4 spring onions, chopped
1 handful of fresh mint leaves,
    roughly torn

ZA'ATAR DRESSING
4 tablespoons extra-virgin
    olive oil
2 teaspoons za'atar, plus extra
    to serve
1 garlic clove, finely chopped
Juice and grated zest of
    ½ lemon
Sea salt and black pepper

1. Prepare the dressing by whisking everything together in a large salad bowl. Season to taste with salt and pepper.

2. Add the salad ingredients to the bowl, toss in the dressing and sprinkle with a little extra za'atar, to serve.

✳ Use It Up

Mint is refreshing but any leftover herbs such as dill, coriander, basil or parsley will work well here.

● Tip

Use a spoon to scoop out the cucumber seeds.

Herb & pak choi salad

If you haven't tried pak choi raw yet, you're in for a treat. Be sure to use fresh pak choi and look out for the baby or smaller heads, which will be less bitter. Cold-pressed sesame oil is delicious and very different from the toasted variety, though you could use extra-virgin olive oil instead. This is best dressed just before serving to keep the leaves fresh and perky. Try it with Korean Chicken (p. 88), Five-spice Fish (p. 121) or any cooked noodles.

Serves 4 as a side

Leaves of 4 large heads of pak choi, shredded

Leaves of 1 large Little Gem or cos lettuce, finely shredded

1 large handful of fresh coriander, roughly chopped

1 large handful of fresh mint leaves, roughly chopped

1 large handful of fresh Thai basil, roughly chopped

4 spring onions, finely sliced

DRESSING

Juice and grated zest of 1½ limes

6 tablespoons sesame oil (not toasted) or extra-virgin olive oil

1 teaspoon raw honey or maple syrup

2 tablespoons tamari

Sea salt and black pepper

TOPPING

1 large handful of almonds, cashews or sesame seeds (or a mixture)

1. To make the topping, heat up a frying pan and dry-toast the nuts or seeds and a little salt for about 1 minute over a medium heat until golden. Keep an eye on them as they'll quickly burn, and toss halfway through cooking.

2. Whisk the dressing ingredients together in a large serving bowl and season to taste.

3. Place the shredded pak choi and lettuce and the chopped herbs in the bowl and mix with the sliced spring onions. Toss in the dressing and top with the toasted nuts or seeds.

✳ Use It Up

Instead of the pak choi you could use finely shredded Chinese cabbage here, or indeed any cabbage, and don't worry if you can't get every type of fresh herb – just use what you've got.

Caprese salad with figs

This is more of a special-occasion salad because of the expensive ingredients. It takes less than five minutes to put together with no cooking needed. Look for ripe Italian figs available in midsummer or the Greek ones, from late summer to autumn. Go for good-quality creamy buffalo mozzarella or burrata, as you will really taste the difference.

Serves 4 as a side or starter

200g rocket or baby spinach
1 handful of fresh basil leaves
4 ripe figs, quartered
200g mixed tomatoes, sliced
1 large ball of buffalo mozzarella or burrata (about 250g), sliced or roughly torn
3 tablespoons extra-virgin olive oil
1 tablespoon balsamic vinegar or pomegranate molasses
Sea salt and black pepper

1. Make a layer of green on a large serving platter by covering it with the rocket and half of the basil leaves.

2. Add the figs, tomatoes and mozzarella in an alternating pattern over the leaves, tucking in the remaining basil leaves throughout.

3. Sprinkle over a little sea salt and pepper. Drizzle over the olive oil and vinegar just before serving.

✳ Use It Up

Swap the balsamic vinegar/pomegranate molasses with apple cider vinegar sweetened with 1 teaspoon of raw honey or maple syrup. As an alternative to mozzarella or burrata, some goat's cheese would work equally well.

California-style kale salad with avocado dressing

For a warmer day, kale is delicious raw. The vinegar and salt in the avocado dressing softens the sliced leaves, which marinates the kale and also makes it easier to digest. If you prefer your kale cooked, steam the leaves or stir-fry them in a little coconut oil or ghee for about three minutes, allow to cool slightly, then toss in the dressing. I always make a double batch of this salad as, unlike other leafy salads, it lasts for two to three days in the fridge. It's also great tossed in a Waste Not, Want Not Bowl (p. 72). And try the dressing drizzled over roughly torn romaine lettuce or with some roasted broccoli or green beans.

Serves 4 as a side

250g kale

AVOCADO DRESSING
Flesh of 1 large, ripe avocado
6 tablespoons water
1½ tablespoons apple cider vinegar
1 large garlic clove, peeled
1 teaspoon mustard
2 teaspoons maple syrup or raw honey
Sea salt and black pepper

TOPPINGS
1 handful of mixed nuts or seeds (such as toasted walnuts or pecans, pumpkin or sunflower seeds)
1 handful of dried berries (such as cranberries or goji berries)

1. Whizz all the dressing ingredients together in a food processor or blender and season to taste.

2. Pull the leaves off the kale stems, then stack the leaves, roll into a cylinder and slice into thin ribbons. Place the sliced kale in a large serving bowl and pour over the dressing. Rub the dressing into the kale and leave for a minimum of 20 minutes to soften.

3. Serve sprinkled with your choice of toppings, to add texture and crunch.

✳ Use It Up

To bulk this salad up into a main dish, add some leftover roasted veg (p. 204), cooked beans, flaked fish or shredded chicken.

Best mixed side salad

This is my go-to side salad: a mixture of crunchy, soft and bitter lettuce leaves tossed in a simple dressing. A side salad should take just a few minutes, so that you never have to worry about getting another dish on the table, but you can add more layers, of course, such as chopped herbs, spring onions or slices of fennel or avocado, or a handful of toasted nuts or dried fruit. Make sure to spin the leaves after you've washed them, so they are dry enough for the dressing to coat them properly, and look out for red chicory, which adds a lovely colour contrast.

Serves 4 as a side

Leaves of 1 butter lettuce,
   roughly torn
Leaves of 1 cos lettuce,
   roughly torn
Leaves of 3 heads of red or
   white chicory

MUSTARD DRESSING
5 tablespoons extra-virgin
   olive oil
Juice of 1 lemon
1 teaspoon mustard
1 teaspoon raw honey
   or maple syrup
Sea salt and black pepper

1. In a wide serving bowl, whisk up the dressing, seasoning to taste with salt and pepper. Add the salad leaves and toss gently, then serve immediately.

Salsa salad

Here all the elements of a fiery salsa are rustically chopped into a salad. It would be delicious with the Coriander & Lime Quinoa (p. 192) or Chicken Fajitas (p. 82), or transform it into a more substantial dish by adding a tin of black beans. Double up and make a big bowl for a party or barbecue, mix the dressing in advance with all the other ingredients (except the avocado), then add the avocado at the end.

Serves 4 as a side

4 tomatoes, diced into 1.5cm
   cubes, or 500g cherry
   tomatoes, quartered
Flesh of 1 large avocado,
   diced into 1.5cm cubes
8 radishes, diced
1 small red onion, finely
   chopped
1 large handful of fresh
   coriander, roughly chopped

DRESSING
1 fresh jalapeño chilli,
   deseeded and finely chopped
   (or to taste)
2 garlic cloves, finely chopped
6 tablespoons extra-virgin
   olive oil
Juice of 1½ limes
Sea salt and black pepper

1. Whisk all the dressing ingredients together in a large serving bowl.

2. Add all the other ingredients, toss to combine and season to taste. Leave to sit for 10 minutes before serving.

✳ Use It Up

Have leftovers at breakfast with a fried egg or use to top a bowl of stew or stir through some cooked quinoa.

● Tip

Always test a jalapeño first: chop off a little and touch with the tip of your tongue to assess its power!

Slaw in seconds

This really is a 'slaw in seconds' if you use a food processor; otherwise it's more like a 'ten-minute slaw' if chopping by hand! Here are two simple slaws for the hot and cold months with a dressing to suit either. Add some texture with some toasted nuts or seeds. I love that a slaw can be counted on to go with anything and everything. My mum will add a splash of tamari, chilli or fish sauce to her coleslaw to, in her words, 'Asian it up' a bit!

Serves 4 as a side

SUMMER COLESLAW
1 small green or white cabbage
   (about 400g)
1 small fennel bulb or
   2 celery sticks
1 large carrot
4 spring onions
1 handful of fresh parsley
   and/or dill

WINTER COLESLAW
1 small red cabbage
   (about 400g)
1 small Savoy cabbage
   (about 400g)
½ small red onion, or 1 leek
1 apple, cored
1 handful of fresh parsley
   and/or dill

DRESSING
200ml natural yoghurt
2 teaspoons mustard
   (or to taste)
2 tablespoons lemon juice
   (summer) or 1½ tablespoons
   apple cider vinegar (winter)
2 tablespoons extra-virgin
   olive oil
1 garlic clove, finely chopped
1 teaspoon raw honey or
   maple syrup
Sea salt and black pepper

1. First chop up the larger vegetables so that they fit through the feed tube of the food processor (if using), then shred all the ingredients for either the summer or the winter coleslaw in the food processor using the grater attachment. Alternatively, chop everything by hand.

2. Whisk all the dressing ingredients together in a large serving bowl, seasoning to taste with salt and pepper. Add the shredded vegetables and herbs and toss to combine.

✳ Use It Up

You can replace the dressing with the Tahini Lemon Drizzle (p. 146), which is just as quick to make.

Hot-smoked trout with a beetroot fennel salad & Scandi-style dressing

This would make an excellent packed lunch. You could use hot-smoked salmon, though my first choice would be either trout, as here, or mackerel. I love oily fish; it's nutritious, cheap and readily available. This Scandinavian-inspired dressing would be great as a creamy sauce with some roasted celeriac or squash. If you don't like dill, simply swap it for parsley or chives.

Serves 4 as a main

2 x 400g tins of lentils (Puy, brown or green), drained and rinsed
1 fennel bulb, trimmed (fronds saved to garnish)
1 pink candy beetroot
1 yellow beetroot
200g watercress or salad leaves
4 hot-smoked trout fillets (total 500g)
1 small handful of fresh dill, chopped, to serve

SCANDI-STYLE DRESSING
4 tablespoons natural yoghurt
4 tablespoons extra-virgin olive oil
1 tablespoon mustard
1 teaspoon raw honey or maple syrup
Juice and grated zest of ½ lemon
Sea salt and black pepper

1. Whisk the dressing for the salad, seasoning to taste with salt and pepper, and pour half into a large bowl. Add the lentils and mix with the dressing.

2. Slice or shave the fennel and beetroots very thinly using a sharp knife or a mandolin or the single blade on a box grater.

3. Spread out the salad leaves on a large serving platter, then pile on the creamy lentils and the fennel and beetroot slices. Flake the fish over, drizzle with the remaining dressing and scatter with the dill and fennel fronds.

✳ Use It Up

I also like this with 400g (about 6 handfuls) of cooked quinoa (p. 150) as a base, instead of the lentils. Black quinoa works especially well and looks wonderful alongside the multi-coloured beets.

BLT salad with asparagus

This is a spring meets summer salad for when asparagus is in season and the warm weather is luring you outside for your lunch break. When asparagus are out of season, make this with green beans or broccoli. This is delicious served cold as a part of a packed lunch or a picnic but also very tasty as a warm dish with the bacon and asparagus straight from the oven and the eggs still hot, yolks oozing. Be sure to use good-quality bacon or swap the bacon for a handful of anchovies or fried halloumi slices.

Serves 4 as a side or starter

6 rashers of bacon
350g asparagus spears, woody ends snapped off
6 eggs
Leaves of 4 Little Gem lettuces
200g tomatoes, sliced (or halved if cherry tomatoes)
Flesh of 1 large avocado, cubed

DRESSING
2 tablespoons chives, chopped
6 tablespoons extra-virgin olive oil
2 teaspoons mustard
2 tablespoons apple cider vinegar
1 teaspoon raw honey or maple syrup
Sea salt and black pepper

1. Preheat the grill to high, or the oven to fan 220°C/Gas mark 9, and line a baking tray with baking parchment.

2. Prepare the dressing by whisking all the ingredients together and seasoning with salt and pepper, to taste.

3. Place the bacon rashers and asparagus spears on the lined baking tray and either grill for 6–8 minutes (turning halfway) or roast in the oven for 10 minutes.

4. Meanwhile, fill a large saucepan with boiling water and cook the eggs on a medium simmer for 6½ minutes. Remove from the pan and leave to cool in cold or iced water before peeling and cutting in half.

5. Place the lettuce leaves, tomatoes and avocado in a large serving bowl, drizzle over half the dressing and gently toss. Roughly chop up the cooked bacon and scatter over, along with the hot asparagus and egg halves, then drizzle over the rest of the dressing to serve.

✳ Use It Up

Use any salad leaf, and add in that bit of leftover cucumber or celery for extra crunch.

Spicy Thai beef salad

This makes a great sharing starter. You could also serve it as a warm salad in the winter with lightly cooked kale instead of salad leaves. Onglet, also known as hanger steak, is a very tasty and affordable cut, but needs to be cooked rare to be at its best, so if you prefer your beef more well done, then go for a rib-eye or sirloin. You could otherwise serve it with grilled mackerel or, for speed, prawns or shredded cooked chicken.

Serves 4 as a side or starter

2 teaspoons coconut oil
1 onglet or rib-eye steak
 (about 250g; at room
 temperature)
3 large carrots, peeled into
 strips or spiralized (p. 273)
3 spring onions, sliced
Leaves of 4 Little Gem lettuces
Sea salt and black pepper

THAI DRESSING
1 fresh red bird's eye chilli,
 deseeded and finely chopped
1 large garlic clove, finely
 chopped
4 tablespoons extra-virgin
 olive oil
Juice of 2 limes
1½ tablespoons fish sauce
2 teaspoons maple syrup or
 raw honey
2 teaspoons tamari or a pinch
 of sea salt

TO SERVE
1 handful of peanuts or
 cashews
1 large handful of fresh herbs
 (such as coriander, mint or
 Thai basil, leaves torn

1. Heat a wide frying pan and add the coconut oil. Season the steak all over with salt and pepper and fry in the melted oil for 1½ minutes on each side for rare (2 minutes on each side for medium rare). Remove to a board to rest for 5 minutes, before cutting the steak into thin slices across the grain.

2. While the steak is resting, whisk the dressing ingredients together in a serving bowl. Add the carrots, spring onions and lettuce to the bowl and toss gently in the dressing, then top with the sliced beef, fresh herbs and nuts.

Lentil salad with garlic yoghurt dressing

This 10-minute salad is great for a lunchbox or as the base for a main dish, bulked out with chopped boiled eggs or beetroot. If serving for a packed lunch or a picnic, keep the leaves on top, rather than mixing in, to stop them wilting. Tinned lentils work well in this dish, particularly Puy lentils, though cooking them from scratch is really simple (see p. 271). I like to keep a jar of this garlic yoghurt dressing in my fridge to serve with beef koftas (p. 94) or to drizzle over roasted vegetables or to enjoy as a fast dip for crudités.

Serves 4 as a side

100g salad leaves (such as rocket, watercress or lamb's lettuce)
2 large handfuls of fresh mixed herbs (such as parsley and mint), leaves roughly chopped
1 small red onion, finely chopped
150g radishes, finely sliced
250g cherry tomatoes, halved
2 tablespoons capers (optional)
2 x 400g tins of lentils (Puy, brown or green), drained and rinsed
½ lemon, cut into wedges, to serve

GARLIC YOGHURT DRESSING
1 small handful of fresh mint leaves
1 large garlic clove, peeled
200ml natural yoghurt
Juice of ½ lemon
4 tablespoons extra-virgin olive oil
Sea salt and black pepper

1. Prepare the garlic yoghurt dressing by finely chopping the mint leaves and garlic and whisking in a bowl with the other ingredients, or by blending everything (apart from the chopped mint leaves) together in a food processor and then stirring through the chopped mint. Season to taste with salt and pepper.

2. Place the salad ingredients in a large serving dish. (I like to make a bed of salad leaves and then pile the rest in the middle.) Add half the dressing and toss together.

3. Serve the salad with the lemon wedges and the rest of the dressing on the side so that people can add more if they wish.

SIDES

'THESE sides are designed to be brought in to complete a meal alongside a dish from Meat and Fish or to enhance a dish from Bowl Food or Vegetable Mains. Equally, they could be enjoyed as a snack or mix and matched, mezze-style, with a dish or two from Salads.'

Why not pair the Ginger, Garlic, Pak Choi & Mushrooms (p. 199) with the Spicy Thai Beef Salad (p. 182), or Buckwheat Naans (p. 191) with Carrot Fritters (p. 200) and a poached egg and Za'atar Salad (p. 168)? Or you could use the Sides as inspiration and build a meal on them. The Roast Cauliflower with Vietnamese Dressing (p. 196) could be mixed with some leftover shredded chicken or squash and a handful of fresh salad leaves to make a great warm salad.

Among the sides here, the herb and citrus quinoa dishes (p. 192) are such useful recipes to have up your sleeve. They go with anything and taste great hot or cold. The Squash Fries (p. 206) make a delicious snack or side to many family favourites, from the Mexican Bean Burgers (p. 000) or Asian Turkey & Carrot Burgers (p. 90) to Chicken Goujons (p. 80) and Japanese Fish (p. 110).

The Chickpea Wraps (p. 190) and Buckwheat Naans (p. 191) are incredibly versatile. Use them as pancakes, wraps, flatbreads, pizza bases, blinis, tacos, tortillas, burritos – you name it! They are so multifunctional that I guarantee you will end up making them on a regular basis. They reheat beautifully, too, and freeze well. For other multipurpose sides look at the Basics section for how to make easy vegetable rice, mash or noodles (pp. 272, 274 and 273) using a wide variety of different vegetables and with no need for any specialised kitchen equipment.

For more sides try:

Roast carrots with pomegranate molasses

Looking for a new way to serve carrots for your Sunday roast? This makes a generous quantity and any leftovers keep well in the fridge. Have them with roast Za'atar Chicken (p. 87), alongside a refreshing salad or with the Spinach & Feta in chickpea wraps (p. 144). Chop up any leftovers and add to cooked quinoa or lentils or incorporate in a quick frittata. If you can't get the pomegranate molasses, substitute with balsamic vinegar or even fresh orange juice.

Serves 4 as a side

1 tablespoon coconut oil
   or ghee
350g small carrots left
   whole, halved or
   quartered lengthways
2 teaspoons maple syrup
1 tablespoon pomegranate
   molasses
3 tablespoons pistachios,
   roughly chopped
Sea salt and black pepper
1 handful of fresh mint leaves
   to serve

1. Preheat the oven to fan 220°C/Gas mark 9. Add the oil to two baking trays and place in the oven for a few minutes to melt.

2. Divide the carrots between the two trays, season with salt and pepper and carefully toss in the hot oil. Spread the carrots in a single layer on each tray.

3. Roast in the oven for about 20 minutes (turning halfway through) until just tender, then add the maple syrup, pomegranate molasses and pistachios. Toss again and roast for another 6 minutes. Serve sprinkled with the mint leaves.

✳ Use It Up

If you don't have pistachios, use any nuts or seeds that you have in the cupboard. Swap the mint for dill, thyme or coriander.

Chickpea wraps with za'atar

Inexpensive and widely available, chickpea (or gram) flour is so easy to work with. These wraps are super versatile too. Use them as flatbreads with the Broccoli, Pea & Feta Dip (p. 214) or Roasted & Spiced Carrot Hummus (p. 213) or in a lunchbox filled with salad, roast veg, shredded chicken or Broccoli Falafels (p. 146). You can either keep the chickpea batter plain and top with a sprinkle of za'atar or harissa as it's cooking, or add spices, seeds or herbs straight into the batter, such as cumin, caraway or sesame seeds, dried rosemary or thyme, or finely chopped garlic or chives. You can make the batter in advance (just give it a stir before you start to cook it) or make a big batch of the wraps to freeze or keep in the fridge (for up to a week), reheating in a dry pan or in the oven.

Makes 8 medium or 12 small wraps

250g chickpea flour
350ml warm water
1 teaspoon sea salt
½ teaspoon black pepper
1½ tablespoons coconut oil
   or ghee
2 tablespoons za'atar or
   2 teaspoons harissa spices
   (or to taste), p. 125
Extra-virgin olive oil, for
   drizzling (optional)

1. Whisk together the chickpea flour, water and salt and pepper and leave to sit for 10 minutes.

2. Melt 1 teaspoon of the oil in a medium-sized frying pan over a high heat. Add 3 tablespoons of the batter to the frying pan, swirling it around to cover the base, and cook for 1½ minutes, sprinkling over the za'atar or harissa, then flip over and cook on the other side for another 30 seconds.

3. Tip the wrap onto a plate, making sure you remove any excess bits from the pan or they'll burn when you cook the next wrap, and repeat – adding a little more of the oil each time – until you have used all the batter. Use two pans for speedier results (see tips).

✳ Use It Up

Turn leftover wraps into tortilla-style chips by slicing them into triangular shapes and reheating in a frying pan with more coconut oil /ghee until crisp.

● Tip

Each wrap will take about 2 minutes to cook. If you're preparing a big batch of these, and want to keep them warm, place the wraps on a plate in the oven, on low, while you finish the rest.

To make 12 small wraps, use a large frying pan and cook two at a time, adding 2 tablespoons of batter per wrap.

Buckwheat naans with garlic butter

I use this basic dough to make really quick pizzas (p. 153), and it is ideal for making naans, which you can spike with different spices and herbs or serve, as here, with lots of garlicky butter. These would be perfect with curry, such as the Dhal (p. 51) or serve sliced up with Hummus (p. 213) or Tapenade (p. 215). They also freeze really well, so either make loads and freeze until needed or just freeze the dough, and enjoy the next time you fancy a pizza!

Makes 8 small naans

200g natural yoghurt
200g buckwheat flour, plus
   extra for dusting
1 teaspoon baking powder
½ teaspoon sea salt
¼ teaspoon black pepper

GARLIC BUTTER
4 tablespoons butter
3 garlic cloves, finely chopped

1. Place all the ingredients in a big bowl and mix together, first with a spoon and then with your hands, until the mixture comes together as a dough.

2. Tip the dough out onto a lightly floured work surface and knead for about 3 minutes to make sure all the ingredients are combined.

3. Next use your hands to roll the dough into a long sausage about 4cm thick, then cut into eight pieces. Roll each piece into a ball and then flatten to about 1cm thick – either with a rolling pin or just with your hands.

4. Get a hot pan going (ideally a griddle pan) and heat each one for 2 minutes on each side until brown and slightly puffy. As you make each naan, place on a plate in a low oven to keep warm while you make the rest.

5. When all the naans are made, add the butter and garlic to the same pan and place over a medium-low heat for 30 seconds until the butter has melted and the garlic has softened. Transfer to a bowl and place in the middle of the table for dipping, or drizzle the garlic butter over each naan to serve.

 Tip

For spiced naans, mix ½ teaspoon each of ground cumin and ground coriander with the other ingredients for the naan dough.

Basil & lemon quinoa

Quinoa makes for a quick and easy side. You could make a big batch of it once a week and use it as a base for other recipes too, such as Chinese Fried Quinoa (p. 140). Here is one of my favourite ways to flavour it up. This version works best with Mediterranean-style dishes such as Ratatouille (p. 62). Coriander & Lime Quinoa would go well with Mexican and Asian food. Delicious hot or cold, any of them would be great in a Waste Not, Want Not Bowl (p. 72), or for breakfast with a fried egg on top.

Serves 4–6 as a side

2 tablespoons butter or ghee
1 onion, finely chopped
2 garlic cloves, finely chopped
200g quinoa, rinsed well
 (ideally soaked first, p. 277)
Juice and grated zest of
 ½ lemon
500ml water or stock/bone
 broth (p. 278)
1 large handful of fresh basil
 leaves, roughly chopped
Sea salt and black pepper

1. In a medium pan, melt the butter and then add the onion and fry over a medium heat for 5 minutes until softened. Add the garlic and fry for a further 30 seconds.

2. Add the quinoa, lemon zest and a pinch of salt and pour in the water, then bring to the boil. Reduce the heat, cover and cook until the liquid has been absorbed and the quinoa is tender (about 15 minutes, or 13 minutes if the quinoa has been sokaed first). Uncover, fluff the quinoa with a fork and set aside to allow to cool.

3. Stir through the lemon juice and fresh basil leaves and season with salt and pepper to taste.

Variations

Coriander & lime quinoa: *Replace the butter/ghee with coconut oil, the lemon with the juice and grated zest of 1 lime and the basil with a handful of fresh coriander leaves and a little jalapeño chilli, if you like.*

Mint, parsley & orange quinoa: *Replace the lemon with the juice and grated zest of ½ orange and the basil with 1 handful of mixed mint and parsley leaves.*

Kung pao green beans

You really need the special kick of Sichuan peppercorns here, and most shops stock them. If you can't get them at the last minute, however, use black peppercorns instead. Green beans freeze well, so I always keep some in the freezer to have on standby for a last-minute stir-fry or a quick curry. This flavour mix would otherwise work well with broccoli, kale, peas, Brussels sprouts, cauliflower or aubergine.

Serves 4 as a side

1 tablespoon coconut oil
  or ghee
1 teaspoon Sichuan peppercorns
4 garlic cloves, finely chopped
A pinch of sea salt
6 spring onions, finely sliced
500g green beans, trimmed
2 tablespoon tamari
2 teaspoon apple cider vinegar
2 teaspoon maple syrup

1. Preheat the grill to high, then add the oil to a baking tray and place under the grill for a few minutes to melt.

2. Meanwhile, roughly crush all the peppercorns into a coarse powder using a pestle and mortar or chop with a knife.

3. When the oil has melted, carefully remove the hot tray and add the crushed peppercorns with the garlic, salt and three-quarters of the spring onions. The ingredients should sizzle in the hot oil.

4. Add the green beans and toss all the ingredients together, then place under the grill to cook for 5 minutes. Remove the tray and toss everything again, then put back under the grill to cook for a further 3–5 minutes until the beans are browned, just tender and starting to blister.

5. Remove from the grill and add the tamari, apple cider vinegar and maple syrup. Toss everything together and put back under the grill to cook for another 2 minutes. Serve with the remaining spring onions scattered on the top.

Heavenly halloumi salad with carrot top pesto

This salty, sweet and spiced hot fried halloumi is served alongside a raw carrot salad with a heavenly carrot top pesto. Carrots are a great all rounder British veg and it's so nice to see them being sold with their gorgeous green tops still intact. These tops, whizzed up with herbs, garlic and almonds, make a lovely pesto or you can fry them up, too, and serve as a side of greens. Enjoy leftover pesto with pasta, on top of grilled fish, or as a dip.

Serves 4 as a side

CARROT TOP PESTO
1 large handful of carrot tops
   (from the 4 carrots below)
1 small handful mint leaves
1 large handful coriander
   leaves and stalks
1 small handful almonds
2 garlic cloves, roughly
   chopped
200ml extra virgin olive oil
Juice of 1 lemon
Sea salt and black pepper

HALLOUMI SALAD
6 large carrots, with carrot
   tops still attached
2 teaspoons ground cumin
1 teaspoon sweet smoked
   paprika
½ teaspoon chilli flakes
1 tablespoon coconut oil
   or ghee
250g halloumi, sliced into
   8 and then into cubes
1 ½ tablespoons maple syrup
Sea salt and black pepper
1 large handful pomegranate
   seeds

1. Clean the carrot tops and chop off the tough stems. Place them, along with all the remaining pesto ingredients in a food processor and pulse until combined. Season to taste.

2. For the salad, use a vegetable peeler to peel the carrots into thick long strips or ribbons or you could use a spiralizer if you have one (p. 273).

3. Heat a frying pan over a medium heat. Toast the cumin, smoked paprika and chilli flakes for a minute until fragrant, stirring constantly.

4. Turn up the heat and add the oil. Fry the halloumi until golden on each side. Add the maple syrup, stir and let bubble for a final 30 seconds to get sticky.

5. Divide the carrot ribbons among the plates, top with the hot fried halloumi, scatter with sea salt and pepper and pomegranate seeds. Drizzle over the pesto and let everyone help themselves.

Roast cauliflower with Vietnamese dressing

Roast cauliflower florets make a great side or starter, even if just simply seasoned. Add a punchy, full-flavoured dressing and the dish will be devoured in a flash! It's delicious served warm or cold. Any extra dressing can be kept in the fridge for up to a week. I love this with some grilled fish or chicken. Leave out the fish sauce if you like, and add a little extra tamari and lime.

Serves 4 as a side

2 teaspoons coconut oil
    or ghee
1 large cauliflower
    (about 900g), chopped into
    small florets
Sea salt and black pepper
1 handful of fresh coriander
    or shiso, roughly torn,
    to serve

VIETNAMESE DRESSING
1 fresh red chilli, deseeded and
    finely chopped (or to taste)
2 garlic cloves, finely chopped
3cm piece of ginger, finely
    chopped
1½ tablespoons maple syrup
Juice of 1 lime
1 tablespoon tamari
1½ tablespoons fish sauce
2 tablespoons water

1. Preheat the oven to fan 220°C/Gas mark 9. Add the oil to a baking tray and place in the oven for a few minutes to melt.

2. Add the cauliflower to the hot baking tray and carefully toss in the hot oil. Place in the oven to roast for about 15 minutes, tossing halfway through, until tender and golden at the edges.

3. Meanwhile, mix all the dressing ingredients together in a bowl – or blend together in a food processor or high-powered blender and season to taste. Spoon over the roast cauliflower and scatter with the fresh herbs to serve.

✳ Use It Up

Try the dressing with all kinds of cooked vegetables – sprouts and broccoli or even roast radishes and carrots – and use it to liven up any leftovers. Use up the thick cauliflower leaves by roasting them too, keep an eye on them and remove halfway through when you toss the florets as they'll cook quicker.

Butter bean mash

This comforting creamy mash is ready in just five minutes. I always go for two cloves of garlic because I love it, but you can adjust to taste. Swap in any of your favourite herbs – sage would go well – or substitute the butter beans for whatever tinned white beans you have to hand. Enjoy this with roast chicken, Spiced Lamb Chops (p. 98) or Fish en Papillote (p. 122).

Serves 4 as a side

1 tablespoon butter or ghee
2 garlic cloves, finely chopped
2 x 400g tins of butter beans,
  drained and rinsed
1 tablespoon lemon or
  lime juice
3 tablespoons hot water
2 tablespoons chopped chives
  or 4 sliced spring onions
Sea salt and black pepper

1. Melt the butter in a wide pan, add the garlic and fry for 30 seconds until softened but not browned. Add the butter beans, lemon juice and the hot water and season with salt and pepper. Turn up the heat and simmer, covered with a lid, for 2 minutes until the beans are hot.

2. Roughly mash the beans in the pan with a potato masher (or whizz in a blender if you want a really smooth mash), stir through the chives or spring onions and taste for seasoning.

Brussels sprouts with Stilton & cranberries

Roasting sprouts is an extra-delicious way of enjoying these lovely little vegetables. You could make a double batch and have the leftovers cold the next day with some baby spinach and leftover quinoa and lentils for a packed lunch. Swap the Stilton for goat's cheese or fried halloumi cubes, if you prefer, and the dried cranberries for fresh pomegranate seeds (added at the end).

Serves 4 as a side

1½ tablespoons ghee
400g Brussels sprouts
  (halved or quartered if large)
1 teaspoon apple cider vinegar
1 handful of dried cranberries
1 handful of walnuts or
  pecans, roughly chopped
100g Stilton
Sea salt and black pepper

1. Preheat the oven to fan 200°C/Gas mark 7. Add the ghee to a baking tray and place in the oven for a few minutes for the ghee to melt.

2. Place the sprouts on the tray, season with salt and pepper and toss in the hot oil. Spread out in an even layer and roast in the oven for 20 minutes (tossing halfway through) until just tender and going golden at edges.

3. Remove from the oven, allow to cool slightly, and stir in the apple cider vinegar, cranberries and walnuts. Crumble over the Stilton to serve.

Ginger, garlic, pak choi & mushrooms

A quick 10-minute side that can be turned into a main dish by adding fried eggs or serving with leftover noodles, quinoa, grilled fish or chicken. This would be a good side to pair with Asian Turkey & Carrot Burgers (p. 90) or Korean Chicken (p. 88). Pak choi is widely available, though this would work just as well with cabbage and other dark leafy greens. Use any type of mushroom.

Serves 4 as a side

1 tablespoon coconut oil
  or ghee
2 garlic cloves, finely chopped
3cm piece of ginger, finely
  chopped
500g mushrooms, roughly
  chopped
4 large heads of pak choi
  (total 500g)
2 tablespoons tamari
Sea salt and black pepper
1 tablespoon sesame seeds or
  chilli flakes, to serve
  (optional)

1. In a wide pan, melt the oil and fry the garlic and ginger over a medium heat for 1 minute.

2. Tip in the mushrooms and fry for 4 minutes until they have released their liquid, stirring occasionally.

3. Slice the end off each of the pak choi, keeping each leaf intact, then add to the pan with the tamari and a splash of water and cook for 2–3 minutes or until the leaves are wilted and the stalks are just tender. Season with salt and pepper to taste and serve scattered with the sesame seeds or chilli (if using).

Quickly pickled veg

This would also work well with chopped cauliflower, peppers, onions or beetroot and whole peeled garlic cloves. It goes really well with Japanese Fish (p. 110).

Serves 6 as a side

½ cucumber
1 carrot
8 radishes or 100g daikon

PICKLING LIQUID
150ml apple cider vinegar
½ teaspoon sea salt
1 teaspoon maple syrup
¼ teaspoon chilli powder
  (optional) or 1 teaspoon
  caraway seeds

1. Thinly slice all the vegetables and place in a sterilised 500ml jar. Add the pickling liquid ingredients and seal with the lid, shake well and leave for 15–20 minutes. Enjoy within a few days and discard the pickling liquid.

Carrot fritters

I first made these easy fritters to use up my last three carrots but now I buy carrots just to make them! Poach an egg and serve on top, or serve with something fresh, such as the Salsa Salad on p. 176, or in a Chickpea Wrap (p. 190) with some slaw. They are delicious, hot or cold, and can be made bite sized if you like, to serve as canapés or fried as one big fritter in a medium-sized pan and sliced up into wedges.

Serves 4 as a side/ Makes 9 fritters

3 spring onions, chopped
1 egg, beaten
2 tablespoons flour
   (such as buckwheat or
   chickpea) or ground
   almonds
1 handful of fresh parsley,
   chopped
1 tablespoon garam masala
1 garlic clove, finely chopped
½ teaspoon sea salt
¼ teaspoon black pepper
3 large carrots (total 400g),
   coarsely grated
1½ tablespoons ghee or
   coconut oil

1. Place the spring onions and egg in a bowl with the flour, herbs, spices, garlic, salt and pepper.

2. Squeeze out any moisture from the carrots and then add them to the mixture.

3. In a wide frying pan, melt 1 teaspoon of the oil, swirling it around the pan to coat. Add 1 tablespoon of the mixture per fritter and fry for 2 minutes on each side until golden. Flatten each fritter gently as it touches the pan, to ensure it is evenly flat and fries uniformly. Aim to cook three fritters at a time and then set aside, adding more oil to cook the next batch.

✳ Use It Up

Add any leftover peas or swap spring onions for that last half an onion in the fridge.

Killer kale

This really does go with everything and is one of the most straightforward and delicious ways to cook kale. Enjoy this freshly cooked or as leftovers to top a soup or stew. You could serve it alongside any of the fish or meat dishes, or use it as the base of a salad or Waste Not, Want Not Bowl (p. 72).

Serves 4 as a side

2 teaspoons coconut oil
  or ghee
3 garlic cloves, finely chopped
1 fresh red chilli, finely
  chopped (or to taste)
400g kale, stalks removed
  and leaves roughly chopped
2 tablespoons water
Sea salt and black pepper

1. In a very wide pan, melt the oil, then add the garlic and chilli and fry on a medium heat for 30 seconds.

2. Add all the kale and a big splash of water and turn up the heat. Give the kale a good stir and fry for 3–4 minutes until tender. Some of the edges will get a bit crispy, but if you prefer them not to, add a few extra splashes of water to 'steam-fry' the leaves, so that they soften rather than crisp up. Season with salt and pepper to taste.

✳ Use It Up

Substitute the kale with chopped cabbage or other leafy greens, or even with frozen peas when you need to turn them into something more interesting.

Broccoli, beans & pine nuts

Broccoli and anchovies go so well together. This makes a great side dish to serve with a Sunday roast or with the Spiced Lamb Chops (p. 98). It would also be delicious mixed with buckwheat noodles, pasta or quinoa, and I often make this for picnics. You can serve it hot or cold and any leftovers could go in a Waste Not, Want Not Bowl (p. 72).

Serves 4 as a side

1 tablespoon butter
  or ghee
3 garlic cloves, finely chopped
4 tinned anchovy fillets
1 large head of broccoli
  (about 500g), chopped into
  small florets
1 x 400g tin of cannellini
  beans, drained and rinsed
1 tablespoon lemon juice and
  1 teaspoon grated zest
Sea salt and black pepper

TO SERVE
3 tablespoons pine nuts
Extra-virgin olive oil, for
  drizzling
Shavings of Parmesan or
  pecorino (optional)

1. In a wide frying pan, dry-toast the pine nuts (to serve) over a medium heat for just under a minute, tossing occasionally to make sure they don't burn and set aside.

2. Melt the butter in the same pan, add the garlic and anchovies and cook over a low heat for 1 minute, breaking up the anchovies with a wooden spoon.

3. Add the broccoli, stirring to coat, then increase the heat to medium, add a good splash of water, cover with either a lid or some foil, and leave to steam for 5 minutes.

4. Stir in the cannellini beans and cook for another 1–2 minutes until the broccoli is just tender and the beans are heated through, then remove from the heat.

5. Add the lemon juice and zest, then season to taste with salt and pepper, drizzle with olive oil and top with toasted pine nuts and the Parmesan (if using).

✳ Use It Up

You could also swap the broccoli for any vegetables from the cruciferous family – cauliflower, kale, cabbage or Brussels sprouts. Add any cooked beans, lentils or chickpeas.

Roast vegetable tray bake

A big baking tray loaded with roasted vegetables is one the simplest ways to cook up a good mixture of different veg and have them ready to go, hot or cold, all week. Roasting vegetables brings out their sweetness; all you really need to think about is selecting and preparing them so that they're ready within a 30-minute time frame. A softer vegetable, like cherry tomatoes or courgettes, will cook quickly, so cherry tomatoes should stay whole and courgettes can be chunkily chopped. Harder vegetables, like swedes, beetroots and celeriac, should be chopped into smaller chunks so they'll cook more quickly. The beauty of a tray or two of roasted veg is that it makes for really easy packed lunches, a Waste Not, Want Not Bowl (p. 72) or as a base for quick leftovers. Try with different dressings (see below) to jazz them up or simply serve with some good-quality extra-virgin olive oil.

Serves 4 as a side

1½ tablespoons coconut oil
  or ghee
Sea salt and black pepper

SUMMER VEG OPTIONS
4 LARGE HANDFULS OF ANY
OF THE FOLLOWING
Spring onions
Cherry tomatoes on the vine
Pepper/aubergine chunks
Courgette chunks
Asparagus spears
Green beans

WINTER VEG OPTIONS
4 LARGE HANDFULS OF ANY
OF THE FOLLOWING:
Squash chunks
Swede/celeriac/beetroot
  chunks
Carrot batons
Onion wedges
Brussels sprouts
Shredded kale or chard leaves

HERB OPTIONS
1 tablespoon dried oregano or
  marjoram (summer)
1 tablespoon dried thyme,
  rosemary or sage (winter)

1. Preheat the oven to fan 220°C/Gas mark 9, then add the oil to one to two baking trays and pop into the oven for 5 minutes to melt. This also preheats the tray(s), which makes the cooking process quicker.

2. Add your selection of summer or winter vegetables and herbs to the tray(s), season with a big pinch of salt and pepper and toss in the melted oil. Spread all the vegetables out in a single layer then roast in the oven for 15 minutes.

3. Remove the baking tray(s), toss all the vegetables together and return to the oven to roast for another 8 minutes (for the summer veg). If using winter veg, at this point add any leafy greens and cook for a final 15 minutes.

4. Serve immediately as is or with your chosen dressing. Keep in the fridge for 2–3 days.

✳ Use It Up

Use up any dressing that you've made from another recipe such as:
Basil Pesto p. 67
Ginger tahini dressing p. 166
Garlic Yoghurt Dressing p. 183
Tahini Lemon Drizzle p. 146
Lemon Herb Drizzle p. 87

Butternut squash fries & spiced ketchup

Grated Parmesan gives a lovely texture to these vegetable fries, but they taste delicious just simply seasoned, so feel free to leave the cheese out. You can follow the same basic recipe for making chips with any root vegetables – celeriac, carrots, sweet potatoes, parsnips, swede or beetroot. The spiced ketchup makes a good amount – any extra can be kept in the fridge for up to a week, and is perfect with fish or Chicken Goujons (p. 80).

Serves 4 as a side

1 tablespoon coconut oil
  or ghee
1 butternut squash (about 1kg)
1 teaspoon dried herbs
  (such as oregano, thyme or
  rosemary), optional
50g Parmesan, grated
Sea salt and black pepper

SPICED KETCHUP
1 tablespoon butter or ghee
2 garlic cloves, finely chopped
6 tablespoons tomato purée
2 tablespoons maple syrup
1½ tablespoons apple cider
  vinegar
1 teaspoon smoked paprika
¼ teaspoon cayenne pepper
4 tablespoons water
1 tablespoon tamari

1. Preheat the oven to fan 220°C/Gas mark 9. Add the oil to two baking trays and place in the oven for a few minutes to melt.

2. Peel the squash only if the skin is really thick, then chop into sections (see tip) and remove the seeds. Slice each section into skinny chips, about 6mm wide and 3cm long.

3. Add the squash chips to the baking trays and sprinkle with the dried herbs (if using). Season with salt (adding less if using Parmesan) and carefully toss in the hot oil, then bake in the oven for 22–25 minutes. Halfway through cooking, add the Parmesan (if using), toss again and return to the oven to finish baking.

4. Meanwhile, make the ketchup. Melt the butter in a saucepan, add the garlic and fry for 30 seconds. Add all the remaining ketchup ingredients, season with salt and pepper, to taste, and simmer for 10 minutes (covered with a lid). Remove from the heat and set aside to cool and thicken.

5. When the fries are ready, combine them on one tray and tuck a small bowl of the ketchup among the fries to serve.

● Tip
Chop the squash at the point where the 'neck' part meets the bottom and then cut each part in half again.

SNACKS, DIPS & CANAPÉS

'**L**IFE can be unpredictable and while it would be great to stick to three nutrient-rich meals a day, there are times when having a good arsenal of snacks to draw upon can be essential to provide a quick energy boost. This chapter includes some very easy, fuss-free snacks for when you're on the go and need a pick-me-up. '

If I'm at home, one of my go-to snacks is a cup of leftover homemade soup or ideally a restorative mug of hot broth (p. 219), especially with miso and an egg stirred in. It is my first choice after exercising or when I need an energy boost. A mug of hot liquid might not sound very satisfying as a snack, but it is seriously delicious and comforting. Do give it a go!

Leftovers also make great snacks and it means everything gets eaten (no waste!). For example, if you've got any smoked mackerel pâté (p. 24) from the day before, or a glass of green smoothie (p. 252) from breakfast, make sure you keep it in the fridge for later. Other really, really simple snacks include ½ an avocado with sea salt and a squeeze of lime or a spoonful of nut butter or tahini on a celery stick or a slice of apple.

If you're hosting a gathering, canapés needn't be daunting! They are really just small bites that people can eat while standing with a drink in one hand. For an easy but stylish option, a vibrant-coloured dip like the Roasted & Spiced Carrot Hummus (p. 213), a simple dip like the Broccoli, Pea & Feta (p. 214), a storecupboard dip like Olive & Black Bean Tapenade (p. 215) or the very quick Cheeky Tzatziki (p. 218), would be perfect. Serve with the Chickpea Crackers (p. 212) or colourful crudités such as cucumbers, radishes, carrots, chicory leaves, fennel, celery or cauliflower and broccoli florets. The Aubergine Pizza Bites (p. 220) would be ideal too and always go down a storm. You can prep them in advance and pop them in the oven to serve. My mantra is to keep things simple. Serve just two canapés – one veggie and one meat or fish – along with a dip and a heaped plate of crudités, and you'll have happy guests and, most importantly, you'll be able to enjoy yourself!

For more snacks & dips try:

Anytime blueberry bake
  Sweets (p. 244)

Buckwheat Naans
  Sides (p. 191)

Carrot Fritters
  Sides (p. 200)

Chickpea Wraps
  Sides (p. 190)

Chocolate chickpea squares
  Sweets (p. 234)

Granola
  Breakfast & Brunch (p. 22)

Parmesan Bites
  Bowl Food (p. 60)

Quick Quinoa Bread
  Breakfast & Brunch (p. 21)

Spinach & Smoked Trout Muffins
  Breakfast & Brunch (p. 25)

Wasabi Pea Dip
  Fish (p. 110)

'Bite size' versions of other recipes

Many of the recipes in this book can be transformed into canapés simply by making them smaller – see below for some ideas.

Beef & Carrot Koftas (p. 94) with Garlic Yoghurt Dressing (p. 183)

Broccoli Falafels with Tahini Lemon Drizzle (p. 146)

Butternut Squash Fries & Spiced Ketchup (p. 206)

Caprese Salad with Figs (p. 172) on sticks

Carrot Fritters (p. 200) with Garlic Yoghurt Dressing (p. 183)

Ginger Fish Burgers (p. 114) with Hoisin Sauce (p. 92)

Mexican bean balls (p. 148) with Guacamole (p. 53)

Parmesan Chicken Goujons with an Avocado Ranch Dip (p. 80)
  or Spiced Ketchup (p. 206)

Watermelon, Feta & Griddled Avocado (p. 162) on sticks

Chickpea crackers

Enjoy these crackers with a dip for a healthy and delicious snack. You can slice the rolled dough into squares or triangles or use a cookie cutter to shape them, but even quicker, and for that rustic look, just bake the dough in one piece and break it up once cooked. The crackers are great made plain, with no additional flavourings, or you can add a tablespoon of dried herbs or spices. Once baked, keep them in an airtight container and pop them in the oven for a few minutes to warm up, if you like.

Serves 6 as a snack

4 tablespoons coconut oil
   or ghee
400g chickpea flour, plus extra
   for dusting
2 teaspoons baking powder
1 teaspoon sea salt
180ml warm water

OPTIONAL EXTRAS
1 tablespoon dried spices
   (such as cumin or paprika)
1 tablespoon seeds (such as
   fennel or caraway)
1 tablespoon dried herbs
   (such as rosemary or thyme)

1. Preheat the oven to fan 180°C/Gas mark 6 and line two large baking sheets with baking parchment. Melt the oil in a small pan.

2. Place the chickpea flour, baking powder, salt and any optional extras in a food processor and pulse once to combine, then add the melted oil and pulse a few times so you are left with a very fine breadcrumb texture.

3. Slowly add the warm water, little by little – just enough so the mixture comes together and forms a dough.

4. On a work surface lightly dusted in flour, knead the dough for a few minutes until it is very smooth. Divide the dough into two and place each piece on one of the lined baking sheets. Cover each piece of dough with another sheet of baking parchment and then roll out the dough, sandwiched between the sheets of paper, to about 3mm thick (or as thin as you can get it).

5. Peel off the paper from the top of each section of rolled-out dough and add an extra sprinkle of sea salt, then bake in the oven for 12–14 minutes until lightly golden. Leave to cool on the baking sheets before breaking into pieces.

Roasted & spiced carrot hummus

Great for using up any leftover carrots, this would also be amazing made with squash or any other root vegetable, such as beetroot, swede or celeriac. The carrots are first roasted to bring out their sweetness and vibrant colour and then blended with other favourite hummus ingredients. The spices make this dip extra delicious; I always add the turmeric whenever there's a chance for its dusky flavour. This makes plenty, so you could serve as a dip with crudités and then enjoy the rest in a Waste Not, Want Not Bowl (p. 72) or as a side with some roast chicken.

Serves 6 as a snack

1 tablespoon coconut oil
   or ghee
4 carrots (total 300g)
1½ tablespoons ground
   cumin, plus extra for
   serving
2 teaspoons ground turmeric
¼ teaspoon cayenne pepper
   (or to taste)
1 x 400g tin of chickpeas,
   drained and rinsed
3 garlic cloves, peeled
4 tablespoons tahini
3 tablespoons lemon juice
3–4 tablespoons water
4 tablespoons extra-virgin
   olive oil, plus extra to serve
Sea salt and black pepper
1 small handful of fresh
   coriander or parsley,
   chopped, to serve

1. Preheat the oven to 220°C/Gas mark 9. Add the oil to a baking tray and place in the oven for a few minutes to melt.

2. Chop the carrots into rounds about 5mm thick (the smaller the better for quick roasting) and add to the baking tray. Sprinkle with spices and carefully toss in the melted oil. Roast in the oven for 20 minutes (tossing halfway through) until the carrots are tender.

3. Place the chickpeas, garlic, tahini and lemon juice in a food processor or high-powered blender. Add the roasted carrots and pulse to mix, then blend, slowly adding the water and olive oil, until the mixture is the right consistency. You may need to add a little more water if the hummus seems too thick.

4. Taste for seasoning, adding a little more tahini or lemon juice, if you like. Transfer to a bowl, drizzle with more olive oil and top with the chopped herbs and a sprinkling of extra cumin. Serve warm or cold and store leftovers in the fridge for 3–5 days.

Broccoli, pea & feta dip

An excellent way to eat more broccoli, with some peas thrown in for sweetness. Serve this with crunchy crudités or Chickpea Crackers (p. 212), or as a side with the Spiced Lamb Chops (p. 98). The peas can be replaced with broad beans, and any fresh herb will do to make this green dip even greener!

Serves 4 as a snack

1 small head of broccoli
  (about 200g), cut into
  medium-sized florets
1 garlic clove, peeled
4 tablespoons water
150g frozen peas
2 tablespoons extra-virgin
  olive oil, plus extra to serve
150g feta, cut into chunks
1½ tablespoons lemon juice
1 small handful of fresh mint
  leaves, finely chopped
Sea salt and black pepper

1. Place the broccoli in a small pan with the garlic and water, cover with a lid and steam over a medium heat for 4 minutes. Add the peas for the final minute. Remove from the heat and drain off any excess water.

2. Transfer to a food processor or high-powdered blender, add the olive oil, feta, 1 tablespoon of the lemon juice and most of the mint leaves.

3. Blend together and season to taste, adding a little more lemon juice, if you like, or a splash of water if the dip seems too thick. Serve with a swirl of olive oil and the remaining mint leaves and keep in the fridge for up to 3 days if not using straight away.

✳ Use It Up

If you don't have any feta, you could swap it for a soft goat's cheese or, for a non-dairy option, use 3 tablespoons of tahini or a nut or seed butter to add creaminess.

Olive & black bean tapenade

This is one of my favourite dips and it's so easy to make. It's also great for preparing in advance as it can be stored in the fridge for three to four days. While black olives would be best, colour-wise, you can use any colour of olives. Serve with a range of crudités or with Chickpea Wraps (p. 190) served as flatbreads.

Serves 6 as a snack

1 x 400g tin of black beans,
   drained and rinsed
120g pitted olives
4 tinned anchovies or
   2 tablespoons capers
1 fat garlic clove, peeled
1- 1½ tablespoons lemon juice
   (or to taste)
1 teaspoon dried thyme,
   oregano or rosemary
Sea salt and black pepper

TO SERVE
Extra-virgin olive oil
Chilli flakes (optional)

1. Place all the ingredients in a food processor or high-powered blender, season with lots of pepper and blitz until mostly smooth but with a few chunky pieces. If it seems too thick, add a couple of tablespoons of water at the end to loosen it.

2. Add a little salt, to taste (bearing in mind that the olives and anchovies are both salty) and serve topped with a drizzle of olive oil and a sprinkling of chilli flakes or extra pepper.

Pictured on following pages, clockwise :
Roasted & Spiced Carrot Hummus;
Broccoli, Pea & Feta Dip;
Chickpea Crackers;
Scotch Eggs.

Cheeky tzatziki

Cucumber is traditionally included in tzatziki, but radishes look so colourful and make a nice change. The cucumber is often grated, but grating radishes is no fun for your fingers, so these are finely sliced instead. It would also make a refreshing side for serving with the Broccoli Falafels (p. 146), Mexican Bean Burgers (p. 148) or any lamb dishes. It will keep in the fridge for up to two days but is best eaten on the same day.

Serves 4 as a snack
300ml natural yoghurt
1 garlic clove, finely chopped
1 small handful of fresh mint
  leaves, finely chopped
2 tablespoons extra-virgin
  olive oil, plus extra to serve
1½ tablespoons lemon juice
15 radishes (total 150g), sliced
Sea salt and black pepper

1. Mix everything together, except the radishes, and season to taste with salt and pepper. Stir in the radishes and serve with a swirl of olive oil and a few extra chopped mint leaves on top.

Buckwheat blinis with spiced feta

These blinis are very easy: you just cook them like mini pancakes, and they make delicious little snacks or canapés. You could top the blinis with anything you like, from Hummus (p. 213) to Mackerel Pâté (p. 24). Alternatively, top with cream cheese and smoked salmon, like the NYC-style Big Blinis (p. 38).

Makes 30 blinis

BLINIS
1 quantity of buckwheat
  batter (p. 38)
1–2 tablespoons butter or ghee

SPICED FETA
100g feta
4 tablespoons natural yoghurt
1 teaspoon harissa powder or
  1 tablespoon harissa paste
1 handful of sun-dried
  tomatoes, chopped
1 tablespoon chopped fresh
  parsley leaves

1. In a large jug, add the buckwheat batter. Melt 2 teaspoons of butter in a large frying pan. Swirl the melted fat around the base of the pan to cover it, then pour any excess into a small jug.

2. Pour out five to six small circles of batter into the pan, each about 5cm wide, and fry over a medium heat for 45 seconds. Flip over and cook for a further 45 seconds on the other side.

3. Repeat with the remaining batter, using more butter as needed, and transfer the cooked blinis to a plate in the oven, on a low heat, to keep warm.

4. Crumble the feta into a bowl, add the yoghurt and harissa and roughly mix with a fork, seasoning to taste with salt and pepper. Top each blini with a heaped teaspoon of the spiced feta, plus some chopped sun-dried tomatoes and a sprinkling of parsley.

Mug of miso egg broth

Restorative and absolutely delicious, this is my go-to snack. The best way to enjoy it is with properly made bone broth, which, happily, is getting easier to buy but is so simple to make yourself (see p. 278). You can serve this simply seasoned with salt and pepper, and leave out the egg if you prefer – though I always add it! Boost the flavour with a spoonful or two of miso, plus a sprinkling of ground spices – or grate in fresh ginger, turmeric or chilli, if you like. Turn this into a hearty meal by adding any leftover veg, cooked chicken, fish or quinoa.

Serves 2

400ml bone broth (p. 278)
2 eggs
1–2 teaspoons miso paste
   (or to taste)
1 tablespoon lemon or
   lime juice
Sea salt and black pepper

OPTIONAL SPICES
½ teaspoon ground ginger
½ teaspoon ground turmeric
¼ teaspoon cayenne pepper

1. Pour the broth into a medium saucepan and sprinkle in any of the optional spices as you bring the broth to the boil. Reduce to a gentle simmer and leave to cook for a few minutes.

2. Crack the eggs into a small bowl, then gently slide them into the simmering broth and poach for about 2 minutes until the whites are just set. Alternatively, crack the eggs straight into the hot broth and stir through. (The eggs will form 'ribbons' that need no further cooking.)

3. Remove the pan from the heat, then place the miso in a small bowl and whisk with a few tablespoons of hot broth from the pan. Pour the mixture into the pan and give a gentle stir, then add the lemon or lime juice and season with salt and pepper to taste. Divide between two mugs to serve.

✳ Use It Up

Making broth is the ultimate thrifty trick. Use up leftover chicken (or any meat) bones, raw bones, and vegetable bits and bobs to make a killer broth.

Aubergine pizza bites

A cross between aubergine parmigiana and a mini pizza, these always get a lot of attention and go in seconds. They take about 20 minutes to prepare and are really simple to put together, but if you're making them for a party, you can prep them in advance and put them in the oven just before serving for the cheese to go golden, then add the basil leaves to garnish. If you had any leftover Pesto (p. 67), a little dollop of this would be delicious on top. Long, slim aubergines are better here because they tend to be less bitter than the larger, fatter ones and slice into smaller, bite-sized rounds. Pictured here with Vodka & Blackberry Mint Sparkler (p. 259).

Makes 12–14 bites

1 tablespoon ghee
2 long and slim aubergines
   (total 250g)
2 tablespoons tomato purée
   or passata
1 tablespoon water
1½ teaspoons dried oregano
   or thyme
1 teaspoon chilli flakes
   (or to taste)
50g Parmesan, grated
Sea salt and black pepper

TO SERVE
1 small handful of fresh basil
   leaves, roughly torn
Extra-virgin olive oil

1. Preheat the oven to fan 220°C/Gas mark 9. Add the ghee to a baking tray and pop in the oven to melt.

2. Cut the aubergines into 8mm thick slices (about 12–14), then toss and brush over the melted oil and arrange in a single layer on the baking tray. Sprinkle over some salt and pepper and bake in the oven for 10–12 minutes, turning halfway through, until softened.

3. Meanwhile, place the tomato purée with water, or passata, in a little bowl with the water, dried herbs and chilli and stir together.

4. Remove the aubergines from the oven and use a teaspoon to spread some of the tomato sauce on top of each aubergine slice. Sprinkle a little of the cheese over each slice and bake for another 8–10 minutes until golden brown, then remove from the oven and top with the ripped basil leaves and a drizzle of olive oil before serving immediately.

✳ Use It Up

Replace the aubergines with courgette slices, or, if you have enough time, make aubergine 'boats' (p. 97) and top with the same mix. Swap the Parmesan with Cheddar, Gorgonzola or feta, or a mixture of any bits of cheese you have in the fridge.

Scotch eggs

Traditionally, Scotch eggs are made with pork mince and are battered then deep-fried. These are oven-baked for easy and fuss-free cooking. You can use any type of mince – pork, beef, lamb, turkey or chicken. The ground almond coating gives a better texture, but you could use chickpea or buckwheat flour if you prefer. I once served a big tray of these, sliced in half, at a birthday party, with Spiced Ketchup (p. 206) and a massive Summer Slaw (p. 177). They went down a storm!

Serves 12 (1 egg half per person) / Makes 6 Scotch eggs

1 tablespoon coconut oil or ghee
7 eggs
400g minced pork
1½ teaspoons dried sage, rosemary or thyme
1 teaspoon mustard
A pinch of garlic powder (optional)
5 tablespoons ground almonds
Sea salt and black pepper

1. Preheat the oven to 220°C/Gas mark 9. Add the oil to a baking tray and place in the oven for a few minutes to melt.

2. Meanwhile, fill a wide, deep pan with boiling water, bring to a medium simmer and cook six of the eggs for 6½ minutes, then transfer to a bowl of really cold (or iced) water and leave for 4 minutes. Carefully peel (they are soft-boiled and so will be a bit squishy!), then blot dry with kitchen paper and set aside.

3. While the eggs are boiling, place the mince in a bowl with the herbs, mustard and garlic powder (if using), season with salt and pepper and mix together.

4. Place the ground almonds in another bowl and season with ½ teaspoon salt and ¼ teaspoon of pepper. Crack the remaining egg into another bowl and beat well.

5. Next assemble the Scotch eggs. Pinch off one-sixth of the meat mixture and use damp hands to flatten into a circle about 4mm thick. Place one soft-boiled egg into the centre of the circle and wrap the mixture all around the egg, flattening as you go and smoothing out the mixture so that there are no cracks. Dip the Scotch egg first into the beaten egg and then into the ground almonds to coat. Transfer to a plate and repeat with the remaining eggs.

6. Place the Scotch eggs on the baking tray and gently roll in the hot oil, then bake in the oven for 20 minutes, turning halfway through, until golden brown all over. Serve warm or at room temperature.

✳ Use It Up

Swap the minced meat for 400g good-quality sausages. Slice lengthways down the casing of each sausage, remove the contents and mix together in a bowl. There is no need to add the other ingredients to the mix as the sausage meat will be seasoned already.

Bombay spice mix

No two Bombay spice mixes are the same, in my experience. Indeed, whatever you add to the mix, you can't go wrong. A curry powder or a garam masala option are given below, but you could substitute with a mixture of whatever spices you have to hand. As in the recipe here, you want a good mix of contrasting flavours and textures – salty, crunchy and spicy, plus a touch of sweetness from the coconut and the dried fruit. Make up a bowlful to top soups and dhals, to serve as easy nibbles for a party or to curl up with on the sofa (preferably not a white one!) for movie night.

Serves 4 as a snack

2 teaspoons coconut oil
 or ghee
100g cashews, chopped in half
100g mixed seeds (such as
 pumpkin and sunflower
 seeds)
1 teaspoon maple syrup
1 handful of tinned chickpeas,
 drained and rinsed
 (optional)
2 tablespoons dried fruit
 (such as raisins and sultanas)
50g coconut flakes
Sea salt and black pepper

(EITHER) CURRY MIX
2 teaspoons curry powder
 (or to taste)
½ teaspoon ground cinnamon
¼ teaspoon cayenne pepper or
 chilli powder (or to taste)

(OR) GARAM MASALA MIX
2 teaspoons garam masala
¼ teaspoon ground turmeric
¼ teaspoon cayenne pepper or
 chilli powder (or to taste)

1. Preheat the oven to fan 190°C/Gas mark 6½. Add the oil to a baking tray and place in the oven for a few minutes to melt.

2. Meanwhile, place the nuts and seeds in a bowl with the maple syrup and chickpeas (if using). Add your choice of spices (either the curry or the garam masala mix) and a good pinch of salt and pepper and toss everything together.

3. Remove the baking tray from the oven and tip the nut and seed mixture into the hot oil. Toss together, then spread out in an even layer and pop in the oven to cook for 8–10 minutes, removing halfway through to toss again and add the dried fruit and coconut flakes.

4. Remove from the oven and allow to cool slightly before serving, or store in an airtight container, such as a glass jar, and serve within a few days. Toast in the oven, if you like, to make it crunchy again.

SWEETS

' **I** ASKED friends and family what their 'desert island' sweets would be. They reeled off cookies, crumble, banoffee pie, ice cream, chocolate mousse, Victoria sponge . . . So I've made them all! You'll find other all-time favourites here too: zingy Lemon & Lime Drizzle Cupcakes (p. 242), crunchy Chocolate Coconut Clusters (p. 235) and Ginger Fruit & Nut Muffins (p. 238), perfect with a cup of tea. '

Different types of flours, including chestnut, quinoa and coconut, are now widely available, making a great alternative to regular flour and they are naturally gluten-free. Because more and more people are baking with them, prices are going down and most supermarkets are now selling them. I've used naturally sweet chestnut flour in my Choc Chip Cookies (p. 230) and it also makes wonderfully silky, thin crêpes. Ground almonds also make an excellent alternative to wheat flour; they are used in all the sponge-based recipes here.

All these recipes are simple, using as few steps as possible. They all use standard baking equipment and can be prepared in 30 minutes or less. For a really quick and easy 'no bake' dessert, try the 'Soft Serve' Banana Ice Cream (p. 231), which you can flavour to your heart's content (that would be rum and raisin for me), and you must try the Little Chocolate Pots (p. 236), my favourite pudding in the whole chapter. These taste and look like a rich chocolate mousse and take just 5 minutes to make before you leave them to set.

We all know that it's a good idea to cut down on refined sugars in all their guises, and one of the best ways to do so is to make and bake your own sweets. You'll notice that I use small amounts of whole-food sweeteners like raw honey, maple syrup and dried fruit to add just enough sweetness. If you're baking for someone with a really sweet tooth, add a touch more sweetness but then cut down the next time and use as little as you can get away with. Both cinnamon and a little sea salt bring out the sweetness in foods, so use these to your advantage. A touch of salt goes so well with chocolate, bringing out the sweetness of the chocolate and adding another dimension of flavour, as you'll find if you try the Chocolate Chickpea Squares (p. 234).

And this wouldn't be a sweet chapter without a proper big cake, so have a look at the Celebration Cake (p. 240), my take on a Victoria sponge. Sandwiched together with cream and fresh strawberries, it is dead easy to make, looks spectacular and tastes divine!

For more sweet treats try:

Chocolate Orange Granola
   Breakfast & Brunch (p. 22)

Perfect Pancakes
   Breakfast & Brunch (p. 36)

Bananarama Smoothie
   Drinks (p. 253)

Mint Hot Choccy
   Drinks (p. 253)

Happiness balls

These divine chocolate truffles are creamy, rich and so quick to make. Using store cupboard ingredients, they take just ten minutes of prep time: five minutes to melt everything together, and five minutes to roll them in different coatings – cocoa powder, desiccated coconut, pistachios and freeze-dried raspberries, finely chopped, look beautiful.

Makes 30 truffles

8 tablespoons coconut oil
8 tablespoons maple syrup
180g cocoa powder
240g cashew nut butter or
   other nut/seed butter
   (p. 276)
A pinch of sea salt

COATINGS
2 tablespoons cocoa powder
2 tablespoons desiccated
   coconut
2 tablespoons pistachios,
   crushed

1. Place the oil in a medium pan with the maple syrup, cocoa powder, nut butter and salt, and melt over a medium-low heat for a few minutes, stirring to combine.

2. Pour into a wide shallow dish – the wider the dish, the faster the chocolate mixture will cool down – and place in the fridge for an hour for the mixture to set. Alternatively, leave in the freezer for 20–30 minutes.

3. When the chocolate mixture has set, remove the dish from the fridge or freezer and use a tablespoon to scoop up pieces of the mixture. Using dry hands, roll each piece into a 2cm ball. If the truffles are too sticky, put them back in the fridge or freezer to harden up a little more.

4. Next prepare the different coatings. Sprinkle the cocoa powder, desiccated coconut or pistachios onto separate plates. Roll the balls in each coating, then enjoy immediately or store in the fridge for up to a week.

● Tip

These would make a wonderful gift: prepare a double batch and fill a jar to give to someone special. Just remember to keep them in the fridge!

Choc chip cookies

Chestnut flour is lovely to bake with – naturally sweet with a distinct nutty flavour. It's easy to use and it makes great soft cookies that are a little more cakey than crunchy. You could leave out the choc chips and add your favourite spices, such as ginger. These can be stored in an airtight container for up to a week and are delicious served warm – you could reheat them in the oven before eating.

Makes 14 cookies

6 tablespoons coconut oil
1 egg
3 tablespoons maple syrup
1 teaspoon vanilla extract
1 teaspoon cinnamon
150g chestnut flour
½ teaspoon bicarbonate
 of soda
60g dark (70%–85%)
 chocolate

1. Preheat the oven to fan 190°C/Gas mark 6½ and line a large baking tray with baking parchment. Pop the coconut oil on the tray and place in the oven for a few minutes to melt. Remove from the oven and allow to cool down slightly.

2. Whisk the egg in a large bowl, then add the maple syrup, vanilla extract and melted coconut oil from the tray. Combine everything together, then add the flour and bicarbonate of soda and mix into a thick dough. Make the chocolate chips either by roughly chopping the chocolate with a sharp knife or by placing it inside some folded baking parchment and crushing it into rough chunks with a rolling pin. Add to the cookie mixture and stir to combine.

3. Divide the dough into 14 pieces, rolling each piece into a ball between your hands, then place on the lined baking tray and flatten into a cookie about 6cm diameter and as thin as possible. Leave a space of about 3cm between each cookie on the tray.

4. Bake in the oven for 7–8 minutes. Remove from the oven and allow to cool slightly on a wire rack before eating. These will keep in an airtight container for 3 days.

Soft serve banana 'ice cream'

Freezing bananas is a great way of using up ripe fruit. Simply chop up a load of peeled bananas and pop in the freezer. They are perfect for making this instant dairy-free 'ice cream' or for adding to smoothies (p. 231). This ice cream is 'soft serve', so enjoy it straight away or keep it in the freezer for up to 20 minutes. If you haven't got frozen bananas, slice some up now and they'll be frozen in 2 hours.

Serves 2

2 frozen bananas (see above)
1 flavouring option (see below)

1. Place the bananas and your choice of flavourings in a food processor or high-powered blender and blitz for 1½–3 minutes, depending on the strength of your processor/blender. In the first 30 seconds, the frozen bananas will start to break down; in the next 30 seconds, they will become crumbly and, in the next minute or so, they will become smooth like ice cream. Halfway through, stop the blender and use a spatula, if needed, to push down any bits from the sides of the machine.

2. Fold through any additional ingredients and serve straight away. Freeze the mixture for another 15 minutes if adding any 'wet' ingredients (see below).

FLAVOURING OPTIONS
Add one of the following flavour combinations with the frozen bananas:

CINNAMON: Blend in 1 tablespoon of nut butter (p. 276), 1 teaspoon of ground cinnamon and 1 teaspoon of vanilla extract.

TROPICAL: Blend in 4 tablespoons of coconut milk, then fold through 1 small handful of desiccated coconut or coconut flakes and the zest of 1 lime. Fold in a few chunks of frozen pineapple, if you like, for a piña colada flavour.

BERRY: Blend in 80g of frozen or fresh berries.

RUM AND RAISIN: Blend in 4 tablespoons of coconut milk, then fold in 1 small handful of raisins soaked for 10 minutes in 1 tablespoon of rum and freeze for 15 minutes.

CHOCOLATE: Blend in 1 tablespoon of cocoa powder and ½ teaspoon of vanilla extract, then fold through 1 small handful of toasted hazelnuts and top with grated dark chocolate to serve.

MINT CHOC CHIP: Blend in ½ teaspoon of peppermint extract or 20 fresh mint leaves, then fold through 20g dark chocolate roughly chopped into chunks.

CARROT CAKE: Blend in 1 small grated carrot and 1 teaspoon of ground cinnamon, then fold through 1 tablespoon of raisins and 1 tablespoon of roughly chopped walnuts or pecans and freeze for 15 minutes.

Banoffee pie in a glass

Layers of crumbly toasted nuts, sliced banana, creamy yoghurt and sweet 'caramel' – a delicious blend of softened dates and almond nut butter. Use any type of nuts that you like and any kind of yoghurt as long as it's good quality and full fat. These are rich so you only need a small glassful to feel satisfied. You can make up just one or two, if you prefer, keeping the rest of the nut mix in a jar and refrigerating the caramel for another night. If you're making them for a dinner party, they're perfect for preparing ahead as they can be kept in the fridge until needed and it gives them time to set.

Serves 4

180ml just-boiled water
200g dates, pitted
1½ tablespoons almond butter
  or other nut/seed butter
  (p. 276)
2 teaspoons vanilla extract
2 large ripe bananas (total
  260g), peeled and sliced
200ml natural yoghurt
20g dark (70%–85%)
  chocolate, shaved

NUT MIX
180g nuts (such as pecans,
  almonds or walnuts)
2 tablespoons coconut oil
A tiny pinch of sea salt
1½ teaspoons ground
  cinnamon

1. Pour the boiling water over the dates and leave to soften for around 15 minutes.

2. Meanwhile, make the nut mix. In a food processor, briefly pulse the nuts, coconut oil, salt and cinnamon. (Don't pulse too much as you want a chunky, nutty base.) Pour the nut mix into a large frying pan and dry-toast over a medium heat for 1–2 minutes, stirring occasionally and keeping an eye on them to make sure they don't burn.

3. Place the dates and the soaking water into the food processor (no need to wash it out first), along with the nut butter and vanilla extract, and blend until creamy and smooth.

4. Divide the crunchy nut mix between the four small glasses, follow with the creamy date mix, then add the banana slices and a generous dollop of yoghurt. Finish with some shavings of dark chocolate. Enjoy straight away or pop in the fridge to set for 1 hour.

Chocolate chickpea squares

A cross between a brownie and a light cake, these chocolatey squares are best enjoyed straight out of the oven, when they're still warm on the inside, cut through with a pop of sea salt. The ingredients are nutrient-dense so slice them up into smaller squares than you might be used to as a little goes a long way and, I promise you, you'll be satisfied!

Makes 9 squares

200g dark (70%) chocolate
7 tablespoons coconut oil
2 teaspoons vanilla extract
4 tablespoons maple syrup
1 x 400g tin chickpeas,
  drained and rinsed
80g ground almonds
1 teaspoon sea salt
3 eggs, beaten
¼ teaspoon baking powder
50g nuts, optional (such as
  hazelnuts or pecans),
  roughly chopped

1. Preheat the oven to fan 200°C/Gas mark 6 and line a 20cm x 30cm baking tin with baking parchment. Fill a medium saucepan with boiling water from the kettle and place on the hob to simmer gently.

2. Place the chocolate, coconut oil, vanilla and maple syrup in a heatproof bowl, set it over the pan, ensuring that the base of the bowl does not touch the simmering water, and leave for a few minutes until everything has melted. Take off the heat and cool.

3. Blitz the chickpeas in a food processor and add the melted chocolate mix.

4. Mix in the ground almonds, salt, eggs, baking powder and nuts (if using).

5. Pour the mixture into the prepared tin, sprinkle a little more sea salt and bake for 15 minutes until it has a lovely crust on top and is still gooey in the middle.

Chocolate coconut clusters

Inspired by the chocolate 'nests' kids make for Easter, these quick little clusters use just four ingredients and are very moreish. They are made with coconut flakes, as coconut and chocolate go so well together, but you could make them with flaked almonds instead, or a mixture of coconut flakes and flaked almonds.

Makes 24 clusters

100g coconut flakes
100g dark (70%–85%)
   chocolate, broken into
   squares
1 tablespoon coconut oil
Sea salt

1. Preheat the oven to fan 180°C/Gas mark 6 and line one or two baking trays with baking parchment.

2. Pour the coconut flakes into one lined tray, spreading them out in a single layer, and toast in the oven for 3–4 minutes until just golden, keeping your eye on them to make sure they don't burn. Alternatively, dry-toast in a wide pan over a medium heat for 1–2 minutes.

3. Meanwhile, place the chocolate and coconut oil in a heatproof bowl set over a pan of simmering water, taking care that the base of the bowl does not touch the water. Stir occasionally until the chocolate has melted.

4. Remove from the heat and then immediately tip in the toasted coconut flakes. Gently stir until the coconut flakes are completely coated in the melted chocolate.

5. Using a tablespoon, scoop up small clusters of chocolate-covered coconut flakes and place them, spaced apart, on the lined baking tray(s). Add a tiny sprinkle of salt to each cluster, if you like.

6. Place in the fridge to chill for 15 minutes until set. Use a pallette knife or thin spatula to ease them off the baking parchment and keep stored in the fridge in an airtight container for up to a week. Serve them straight from the fridge, as they will start to melt after about 20 minutes.

Little chocolate pots

These lovely little pots are not only rich and smooth, they use just five ingredients and take only five minutes to make. They are perfect for preparing ahead of time as they need to set in the fridge, then all you need to do is pull them out at pudding time and grate over a little chocolate to serve. You can use any type of milk here. Nut milk (p. 276) makes the mixture moussier and lighter. Coconut milk makes it really rich and quite thick but without tasting coconutty. These pots will keep, covered, in the fridge or freezer for a few days. If freezing, allow to defrost for 40 minutes before serving.

Serves 4

180ml any milk
140g dark (70%–85%)
   chocolate, broken into
   squares
3 tablespoons maple syrup
1 egg
1 teaspoon vanilla extract

TO SERVE (OPTIONAL)
Sea salt flakes
1 handful of fresh raspberries
   or cherries or a mixture

1. Gently heat the milk in a saucepan for about 45 seconds until hot all the way through.

2. Place 120g of the chocolate in a high-powered blender or food processor with the maple syrup, egg and vanilla extract.

3. Very carefully pour a quarter of the hot milk into the blender or food processor (or use a ladle, if you prefer) and blend until smooth, then repeat, adding a quarter of the milk at a time, until all the milk is combined and the mixture is silky smooth. (You need to add the hot milk slowly so that it doesn't scramble the egg.)

4. Pour into four small ramekins or glasses and leave in the fridge for a minimum of 1½ hours, or 1 hour in the freezer, to set.

5. When you're ready to serve, grate over the remaining dark chocolate or top with a sprinkling of sea salt flakes or a few fresh raspberries or cherries.

● Tip

If using coconut milk, you'll need the full-fat kind, which tends to separate in the tin, so pour it out, give it a stir and measure out 180ml for this dish, then use the rest in soups or smoothies.

Ginger fruit & nut muffins

This combines a ginger cake with a fruit cake to make gorgeous spiced muffins. I adore ginger so I really amp it up here, but you can play around with the spices and use lemon instead of orange, if you prefer. Pick and mix the dried fruit and nuts as much you like, using raisins, sultanas, dried cherries and chopped dates, for instance, or walnuts, cashews and macadamia nuts. This makes 12 muffins, so you could freeze half, defrost and then pop in the oven at a later date to warm through.

Serves 12

5 tablespoons coconut oil
350g ground almonds
¼ teaspoon sea salt
¾ teaspoon bicarbonate
  of soda
3 tablespoons ground ginger
1 tablespoon ground
  cinnamon
1 teaspoon mixed spice
100g mixed dried fruit
100g mixed nuts, roughly
  chopped
4 eggs
1 tablespoon maple syrup
1 tablespoon vanilla extract
1 tablespoon grated orange
  zest and 1 tablespoon
  orange juice

1. Preheat the oven to fan 190°C/Gas mark 7.

2. In a 12 hole muffin tin, put your coconut oil in one hole and place it in the oven to melt. Remove from the oven and allow to cool slightly.

3. In a large bowl, combine the ground almonds, salt and bicarbonate of soda, then stir in the spices, dried fruit and nuts. Make a hole in the middle of the dry ingredients, crack in the eggs, and whisk together, then add the maple syrup, vanilla extract and orange zest and juice. Pour in the melted coconut oil and stir everything together until well combined.

4. Line your muffin tin with muffin cases and distribute the batter evenly among the 12 cases. Bake in the oven for 12–15 minutes until each muffin is set and lightly browned on top, then alllow them to cool for 10 minutes before serving warm with butter and a cup of tea.

Roasted fruit with cardamom & ginger yoghurt

Delicious with a mixture of stone fruit, such as plums, peaches, apricots or nectarines, or try chopped apples and pears in the autumn. Be sure to get fruit that is ripe. Any leftovers would be great for breakfast. Use the roasted fruit, hot or cold, to top pancakes (p. 36) or porridge (p. 18), and try the cardamom and ginger yoghurt with granola and fresh fruit

Serves 4

2 tablespoons butter or
   coconut oil
Juice of 1 orange
12 mixed stone fruit, halved
   and pitted

**CARDAMOM & GINGER
YOGHURT**
3cm piece of ginger, grated
250ml natural yoghurt
Seeds of 2 cardamom pods,
   crushed, or ¼ teaspoon
   ground cardamom
1 teaspoon raw honey
   (optional)
Grated zest of 1 orange

1. Preheat the oven to fan 200°C/Gas mark 7. Place the butter in an ovenproof dish and pop it in the oven for a few minutes to melt.

2. Remove the dish from the oven, add the orange juice to the melted butter. Add the fruit and toss to coat.

3. Spread the fruit out, skin side down, in the dish and roast in the oven for 20 minutes until the fruit has softened.

4. Meanwhile, make the cardamom and ginger yoghurt. Squeeze the grated ginger into a bowl to make about 1 teaspoon of ginger juice (see tip below), then add the yoghurt, cardamom and honey (to sweeten, if you like). Sprinkle the orange zest over the bowl of yoghurt and serve with the roasted fruit.

● Tip

Ginger juice – so much easier than it sounds! It simply means grating ginger and then squeezing it in your fingers. It produces the most delicious juice that is wonderful in salad dressings or marinades. Discard the ginger flesh once juiced, or keep and add to a stir fry. Zest the orange first before you slice and juice it (as it makes it much easier to get the zest).

Apple & blackberry crumble

Quinoa flakes make a great alternative to oats in this crumble, and you use them in just the same way. A crumble is such a versatile dish: you can change up the fresh fruit and the type of nuts you use in the topping – pecans and pear would make a wonderful variation. Serve warm with a spoonful of Soft Serve Banana 'Ice Cream' (p. 231) or a dollop of Cardamom & Ginger Yoghurt (p. 239).

Serves 4

4 large apples (total 500g; such as Cox or Braeburn)
1 teaspoon ground cinnamon
1 tablespoon maple syrup
150g fresh or frozen blackberries

TOPPING
140g quinoa flakes
20g walnuts, roughly chopped
1 teaspoon ground cinnamon
A pinch of sea salt
50g butter or coconut oil, cold and diced
4 tablespoons of maple syrup
20g nuts or seeds (such as flaked almonds, coconut flakes or pumpkin seeds)

1. Preheat the oven to fan 220°C/Gas mark 9.

2. Halve and core the apples, then dice into 2cm cubes. Place in a 30cm ovenproof dish, mix in the cinnamon and maple syrup and bake in the oven for 12 minutes (mixing halfway through) until the apples are starting to soften. Remove from the oven.

3. Meanwhile, make the crumble topping. In a medium bowl, mix the quinoa flakes, walnuts, cinnamon and salt, then rub in the butter and maple syrup until you have a breadcrumb-like texture.

4. Nestle the blackberries among the softened apples and cover with the crumble mix. Sprinkle with the nuts or seeds and bake in the oven for 12–15 minutes until the topping is golden.

✳ Use It Up

This is also a great way of using up any ends of nut and seed packets you may have lurking in your store cupboard – just sprinkle them over the crumble before baking for extra crunch.

Lemon & lime drizzle cupcakes

If you love citrus puddings, these cupcakes are for you. They have a lovely spongy texture thanks to the ground almonds. You can adjust the amount of glaze to suit you, but I like my drizzle cakes to be really moist and tangy. Great for kids and adults alike!

Makes 12 cupcakes

4 tablespoons coconut oil
250g ground almonds
½ teaspoon bicarbonate
  of soda
Juice and grated zest of
  1 lemon and 1 lime (see tip)
5 tablespoons maple syrup
2 teaspoons vanilla extract
3 eggs
50ml any milk

GLAZE
1 tablespoon coconut oil
1 tablespoon maple syrup
Juice and grated zest of
  1 lemon and 1 lime

1. Preheat the oven to fan 160°C/Gas mark 4 and line a 12-hole muffin tin with paper cases. Melt the coconut oil in a small saucepan, then remove from the heat and leave it to cool for a few minutes so it doesn't scramble the eggs.

2. Meanwhile, combine the ground almonds and bicarbonate of soda in a large bowl. Add the citrus juice and zest, maple syrup, vanilla extract and melted coconut oil and mix together well. Make a hole in the centre, crack in the eggs and whisk together, then pour in the milk and stir everything together.

3. Use a tablespoon to divide the batter among the muffin cases so that each one is three-quarters full. Use the back of the spoon to smooth the tops and then bake in the oven for about 18 minutes until golden.

4. Meanwhile, using the same small saucepan, gently heat the glaze ingredients together for 30 seconds. Remove from the heat and leave to stand, then taste and add more citrus juice, if you think it needs it.

5. When the muffins are out of the oven, leave them in the tin and use a skewer to prick holes in each cupcake. Pour over the glaze so that the cakes can absorb it as they cool.

● Tip

When grating the lemon and lime rind, make sure you use unwaxed lemons and limes. Avoid removing the pith with the zest as it has a bitter taste.

Any time blueberry bake

A really simple recipe to make on a Sunday night to enjoy for breakfast, pudding or snacks throughout the week. I love a piece of this for breakfast on the go, or a smaller portion as a snack or pudding. This bake would also work well made with raspberries, blackberries or cherries, halved and pitted. Enjoy it cold or serve warm with a dollop of yoghurt or 'Soft Serve' Banana Ice Cream (p. 231).

Makes 6 or 9 squares

3 tablespoons coconut oil
200g ground almonds
3 tablespoons maple syrup
½ teaspoon bicarbonate of soda
1 teaspoon lemon juice
Grated zest of ½ lemon
1 teaspoon vanilla extract
3 eggs
300g fresh blueberries

1. Preheat the oven to fan 180°C/Gas mark 6 and line a 20cm square baking tin with baking parchment. Add the oil to the lined tin and pop it in the oven for a few minutes to melt, then remove from the oven and allow to cool slightly.

2. In a large bowl, combine all the remaining ingredients except the eggs and blueberries. Make a well in the middle, crack in the eggs and whisk together, then mix in before stirring through the melted oil.

3. Pour the mixture into the prepared tin and sprinkle the blueberries over the batter, nudging them most of the way into the mixture. Bake in the oven for 18–20 minutes until firm in the middle and just golden on top. Cut into squares (larger ones for breakfast and smaller ones for a snack) and serve warm or leave to cool and eat on the go.

Celebration cake

I end up making this vanilla sponge cake every other week. There's always a birthday or some other reason to celebrate and I'm happy to whip it up at short notice because it takes just 20 minutes in the oven. I'm being a bit naughty having this cake here, as including cooling time it does exceed the 30-minute mark. But, after one bite, you won't regret those extra few minutes! I've gone for fresh strawberries and raspberries, but you can swap with any type of berry or use a good-quality sugar-free jam instead.

Serves 8–10

FOR THE SPONGE LAYERS
250g ground almonds
250g butter (at room
    temperature), plus extra
    for greasing
4 eggs
1¼ teaspoons baking powder
2 teaspoons vanilla extract
3 tablespoons maple syrup

BERRIES AND CREAM
600ml whipping or
    double cream
1 teaspoon vanilla extract
250g fresh strawberries,
    halved if large
250g fresh raspberries
1 tablespoon raw honey
    (or to taste)

1. Preheat the oven to fan 190°C/Gas mark 6½, then grease two 20cm round sandwich tins with oil and line each of the bases with a circle of baking parchment.

2. In a food processor, or in a large bowl using an electric whisk, mix all the ingredients for the sponge layers until combined. Alternatively, melt the butter or oil in a saucepan and then add the remaining ingredients in a large bowl.

3. Divide the mixture evenly between the prepared tins and gently smooth the surface of each cake, then place on the middle shelf of the oven and bake for 18–20 minutes until golden brown, springy to the touch and coming away from the edges of the tin. Set aside to cool for 5 minutes in the tin, then carefully turn out both layers onto a wire rack to finish cooling.

4. When ready to serve, whisk the cream briskly with the vanilla extract until stiff and then spread half over each sponge layer. Add half of the berries to each layer and place one on top of the other to make a sandwich.

✳ Use It Up

In the winter, simmer frozen berries down into a thick compote, sweetened with a little honey or maple syrup, to use instead of the fresh fruit.

DRINKS

' THIS chapter is split into smoothies, hot or iced lattes and shakes, spiced invigorating teas, and a couple of refreshing cocktails. Sometimes drinks are an afterthought to good food, but they do play an important part in kicking off a meal and are central to any celebration. '

Like soups, smoothies and juices are a brilliant way to take in a lot of nutrients, if you're not used to eating lots of salads and veggies. I've given a few options for smoothies, and one green juice (p. 252), but feel free to use them as a guide. I don't believe in eating or drinking anything you don't like (even if it's healthy), so adjust them to suit your own taste buds. You may prefer to use a little more fruit to start with and gradually increase the greens as you get used to them. Just make sure to wash everything well and try to buy organic greens, if you can. You can vary the portion sizes, too; enjoy a big glass for breakfast on the go, or a small glass for a snack.

I don't drink juices and smoothies every day and I don't have them in place of whole vegetables. They make a great snack, however, and when you're in a rush, a well-made and well-balanced smoothie provides a good portable breakfast. You can vary the portion sizes, too: enjoy a big glass for breakfast on the go or a smaller portion for a snack at other times of day.

You'll see that in the drink recipes, as in my food dishes, I use a lot of herbs and spices, fresh and ground. Not only do they make drinks taste better, every herb and spice has its own special nutritional properties. I especially love cinnamon, turmeric, ginger and mint. Herbs and spices also have the added benefit of masking any bitterness in greens, which is worth bearing in mind as a way of getting used to the taste.

I love to make cocktails at a dinner party. Give my two favourite recipes a try, which can be easily doubled or trippled for a crowd. Make the cocktails in a large jug ahead of time and them simply add ice and garnishes when your guests arrive.

Making smoothies

You can use a high-powered blender or food processor for making smoothies. Blenders have liquid measurements marked on the side, so start by measuring the liquid, then add all the other ingredients. It generally helps to add harder ingredients first, such as frozen bananas or ice cubes, and then finish with softer ingredients, such as herbs or spinach leaves.

Juicing

You need about 1kg fresh produce for 500ml juice. When I juice at home, I use a masticating juicer to get the most out of my produce and I keep it simple with six ingredients or fewer. Wash all the ingredients well, chopping fruit and vegetables to the right size to fit your juicer.

Handy swaps

If you're caught short, below are a few handy swaps for ingredients that pop up in a number of the drinks in this chapter. They're not the same, but still handy to have up your sleeve.

IF YOU NEED . . .	SWAP WITH . . .
100ml coconut milk	1 tablespoon coconut oil + 100ml water
½ frozen banana	½ fresh banana + 1 handful of ice cubes
2cm piece of ginger/turmeric	¾ teaspoon ground ginger/turmeric
1 lemongrass stalk	1 teaspoon dried lemongrass

Green go-getter smoothie

This is my go-to smoothie. If you're new to green smoothies, you could start off with less spinach. The fresh mint balances all the 'greenness', and you can add a small apple for a touch of sweetness, if you like. Otherwise, simply adjust to your liking – a good green smoothie should taste delicious, not like medicine! And don't feel you need to measure anything exactly. I've always got fresh ginger to hand, and you can also keep it in the freezer, but ground ginger is a great fallback and gives that kick you need in the morning.

Serves 2–4

600ml water
Juice ½ lemon or 1 lime
1 handful of ice cubes
3cm piece of ginger
Flesh of 1 avocado
½ frozen banana
2 large handfuls of baby
    spinach
15 fresh mint leaves

1. Place everything in a high-powered blender or a food processor and blend until smooth. Pour into glasses to serve.

Just green enough juice

This juice has just enough greenness from the leafy greens, along with the natural sweetness of the apple and a refreshing hit from the ginger, fennel and cucumber. If you're just getting started with green juices, try baby spinach first. This recipe is just a guide, so if you can't get fennel, add another couple of celery sticks and use different greens.

Serves 2

1 apple
2 celery sticks
1 large cucumber
1 small fennel bulb
3cm piece of ginger
1 large handful of kale or
    spinach
Juice of ½ lemon

1. Juice everything together and pour into glasses to serve.

Bananarama smoothie

This smoothie is rich in good fats from the nut/seed butter and tastes delicious. Spirulina is packed with nutrients but has a strong and powerful smell and flavour, so start off with just a little. In a recipe like this, you won't taste it as it's offset by the banana and the cinnamon, which adds sweetness while helping to balance blood-sugar levels. If you prefer, swap the spirulina for a big handful of fresh leafy greens such as spinach, or swap the frozen banana for a fresh one, adding a few ice cubes.

Serves 2–4

600ml water
1 large frozen banana (p. 23)
1 tablespoon coconut oil
1½ tablespoons nut/seed
   butter (p. 276)
1 teaspoon ground cinnamon
2 teaspoons chia seeds or
   flaxseeds (optional)
1½ teaspoons spirulina
   powder (optional)

1. Place everything in a high-powered blender or a food processor and blend until smooth. Pour into glasses to serve.

Mint hot choccy or mint choc shake

I've added a touch of fresh mint to this chocolate drink as I love minty choc flavours, but leave it out, if you prefer, and replace with vanilla extract or a little orange extract for that chocolate orange taste. Served hot, these are rich and short cups of hot chocolate, but if you'd prefer a big mugful, then simply add another 100ml of water. Served as a cold shake, this makes a refreshing mid-afternoon pick me up.

Serves 2

1 tablespoon cocoa powder
½ teaspoon ground cinnamon
5 fresh mint leaves
2 tablespoons cashew butter or
   nut/seed butter (p. 276)
350ml hot or cold water

TO SERVE (OPTIONAL)
1 tablespoon maple syrup or
   raw honey
Cocoa powder, for dusting
1 handful of ice cubes

Mint hot choccy: Place all the ingredients except the water in a pan, add 2 tablespoons of the hot water and mix into a smooth paste, then whisk in the rest of the water. Gently heat through for a few minutes. Divide between small cups, add the maple syrup to sweeten, if you like, and sprinkle over some extra cacao/cocoa powder to serve.

Mint choc shake: Place all the ingredients, including the cold water and maple syrup, in a food processor or high-powered blender and whizz until smooth. Add the ice cubes to the food processor/blender before blending, or add to serve.

Turbo turmeric lime tea (hot or iced)

There are so many great tea blends out there, but I can't find one to top this recipe, thanks to its big flavour and the boost of energy it gives you. I drank a lot of it while I was writing this book. It's refreshing and full of spices, while the ginger and black pepper have a kick that keeps me going! Use fresh ginger and turmeric, if you prefer and enjoy it hot or chilled. It's also delicious as a mixer if you want to add a splash of vodka!

Serves 4

1 teaspoon ground turmeric
1 teaspoon ground ginger
1 teaspoon ground cinnamon
Seeds of 2 cardamom pods, crushed, or ¼ teaspoon ground cardamom
¼ teaspoon black pepper
600ml just-boiled water

TO SERVE
1 tablespoon lime or lemon juice
A squeeze of raw honey (optional)
1 handful of ice cubes (optional)
Slices of lemon or lime (optional)

1. Add all the spices to a large teapot, pour over the water, give a stir and brew for 5 minutes. Alternatively, place all the ingredients in a medium saucepan and simmer gently, with a lid on the pan, for 10 minutes.

2. Strain the mixture, if you like, add the lime or lemon juice and the honey (if using to sweeten) and serve hot. Alternatively, chill in the fridge and serve with ice cubes and a few slices of lemon or lime as iced tea.

3. Return the strained ingredients to the teapot and continue to top up with boiling water to re-brew the mixture.

 Tip

Turmeric can stain your cups yellow over time, so use heatproof glasses or keep special mugs and a teapot for this tea if you drink it regularly!

Pictured on previous pages, left to right:
Turbo Turmeric Lime Tea;
Green Go-Getter Smoothie;
Just Green Enough Juice.

Mint tea with ginger & lemongrass (hot or iced)

While matcha and turmeric tea are great for waking you up in the morning, I find mint tea more calming and hence perfect for an afternoon cuppa. A simple tea made with fresh mint is always a winner and good for digestion, but it's even tastier brewed with ginger and lemongrass. It's handy to keep fresh ginger and lemongrass in the freezer, but if you don't have the fresh ingredients, you can swap with ¾ teaspoon of ground ginger and 1 teaspoon of dried lemongrass.

Serves 4

1 handful of fresh mint
  (leaves and stalks)
3cm piece of ginger, grated or
  finely chopped
1 lemongrass stalk, finely
  sliced
400ml just-boiled water

TO SERVE
1 tablespoon lemon or
  lime juice
A squeeze of raw honey
  (optional)
1 handful of ice cubes
  (optional)

1. Add the mint, ginger and lemongrass to a large teapot, pour over the water and brew for 15 minutes. Alternatively, place all the ingredients in a medium saucepan and simmer gently, with a lid on the pan, for 10 minutes.

2. Strain the mixture, add the lime or lemon juice and honey to sweeten, if you like, and serve hot, or chill in the fridge and serve with ice cubes as iced tea.

3. Return the strained ingredients to the teapot and continue to top up with boiling water to re-brew the mixture.

✳ Use It Up

This is a great way to use up mint stalks from other mint recipes where you just need the leaves.

Grapefruit & cucumber gin fizz

This is my kind of simple summer cocktail – so refreshing, and lovely with freshly squeezed pink grapefruit juice. If you don't fancy the gin, add more sparkling water. I like my drinks tart, but you can mix in a little raw honey, if you prefer. You'll need 1 small, juicy grapefruit for this or you can swap it for 1 large orange or blood orange when they're in season.

Serves 2

½ cucumber
4 fresh basil leaves
8 ice cubes
Juice of ½ lime
60ml fresh grapefruit juice
60ml gin
1 teaspoon raw honey
   (optional)
80ml sparkling water

1. Use a vegetable peeler to peel the cucumber into six ribbons, then divide between two glasses, along with the basil leaves and ice cubes.

2. Add the remaining ingredients to a jug and stir well before dividing between the glasses to serve.

Vodka & blackberry mint sparkler

Mixologist tip! I used to work in restaurants, where I was taught to pop fresh mint leaves in one hand and gently smack my hands together to release the flavour. I love this with mint in the warmer months, and later in the year it's delicious with a small sprig of rosemary instead.

Serves 2

6 fresh mint leaves
6 blackberries
Juice of ½ lemon
1 teaspoon raw honey
  (or to taste)
8 ice cubes
60ml vodka
100ml sparkling water

1. Divide four of the mint leaves and four of the blackberries between two glasses, along with the lemon juice and honey. Muddle them together and add the ice cubes.

2. Divide the vodka between the glasses, top up with the sparkling water and stir, then garnish with the remaining mint leaves and blackberries.

● Tip

If you like, let your vodka, blackerry and mint mix infuse for 10 minutes then strain the bits and top with sparkling water and ice cubes to finish.

STORE CUPBOARD

The vast majority of the ingredients in these recipes are available from your local shops and the supermarket. For the remaining specialist ingredients and for competitive prices, check your local health-food shops and look online. Cooking every day is so much easier when you've got your quality staples, so I recommend bulk ordering online with a friend or family member. You will save money on produce, especially nut products, such as ground almonds or nut butters. I like to do a quick monthly scan of my cupboards and freezer to ensure I keep them well stocked and therefore only need to buy fresh ingredients on a weekly basis.

If you haven't done one in a while, have a quick and satisfying spring clean of your cupboards. Throw out anything that is old – I'm talking months, not just a few weeks past its expiry date – even if it's a healthy dried ingredient like nuts or seeds. Dried herbs and spices go stale after six months, especially once the bottle or package has been opened, so you won't get their full flavour. Keep any glass jars and sterilise them before using them to store spices, herbs, flour and other items for a nicely organised and user-friendly cupboard. Or use them to store homemade dressings or pesto and keep them in the fridge.

Ingredients

NATURAL FATS

Butter: Buy grass-fed, unsalted butter and use in baking and low-temperature cooking such as scrambled eggs or to make creamy mash and add richness to dishes.

Ghee (clarified butter): Use for frying and roasting.

Extra-virgin olive oil: Use in dressings, dips, pesto and hummus and for drizzling over soups and other dishes at the end to serve.

Coconut oil: Add this to smoothies and use for baking, frying and roasting. Look out for the type labelled 'virgin'.

Toasted sesame oil: Use in very small amounts to add big flavour.

CONDIMENTS

Sea salt: Seasoning is important to the taste of the dish and the quality of your sea salt can make all the difference!

Black pepper: For a better flavour, buy whole peppercorns and use a grinder.

Tamari: A fermented wheat-free soy sauce that adds depth to cooking. Use like soy sauce in Asian dishes, sauces and dressings, bearing in mind that it is often stronger and saltier, so you won't need as much. If your tamari is labelled 'double-strength, then halve the amount and taste, and adjust accordingly. '

Apple cider vinegar: Use this just like other kinds of vinegars – in dressings or in soups and stews to add brightness to a cooked dish. Check the label to buy the raw (unpasteurised) and unfiltered variety sometimes classified as 'with the mother' and which is cloudy when you shake it.

Miso paste: Unpasteurised, properly fermented and best added at the end of cooking for its delicious umami flavour. Different brands will have different levels of salt so please just adjust to taste.

Vanilla extract (not essence): Use for baking, drinks and in porridge.

Mustard: Use any type to add to dressings, roasting meat and for cooking vegetables.

Fish sauce: Look for sugar-free.

Seaweed (dried): If you haven't used seaweed – such as nori (used in sushi), wakame or arame – try adding it to soups and stir-fries. While seaweed is not essential in any of these recipes, consider getting some as it is rich in minerals and adds an incredible sweet or smoky flavour.

TINS (BPA-FREE) & JARS

Check labels to ensure the contents are salt-free. Quality tins of cooked legumes are very convenient, but see p. 271 for how to cook dried beans and lentils at home. It's cheaper and the texture is even better.

Cooked beans: Most beans – cannellini, haricot, aduki, butter beans or black beans – can be used interchangeably in these recipes.
Cooked lentils: Lentils – Puy, brown or green – can be used interchangeably in the recipes.
Cooked chickpeas
Chopped tomatoes
Coconut milk (full fat)
Nut or seed butters (including tahini): Go for the raw kind and not roasted and salted. See also p. 276 for making your own.
Tomato purée
Olives (unpitted): Green or black olives can be used interchangeably in the recipes. Make sure to buy olives that are naturally black and not dyed!

FLOURS

The following are used in these recipes for savoury cooking and sweet baking:

Buckwheat flour
Chickpea (gram) flour
Chestnut flour
Quinoa flour
Ground almonds

QUINOA & BUCKWHEAT

These should be soaked, ideally before cooking as it aids digestion and reduces cooking time (p. 277). But don't worry if you're not able to soak them; just be sure to rinse them thoroughly before cooking.

Quinoa: High in protein, quinoa comes in three varieties, white (pearl), black or red. Use the whole seed for cooking like rice and using in savoury dishes; flakes for porridge and baking; and flour for making bread (p. 21).

Buckwheat: Like quinoa, buckwheat is a seed rather than a wheat grain, as its name implies. Use groats as an alternative to rice or couscous and flour for making naans, pizzas and blinis.

NOODLES & PASTA

There is a good range of easy-to-find alternative noodles and pasta these days, including varieties made with buckwheat, quinoa, mung beans or chickpeas. As with all processed foods, look for those containing as few added ingredients as possible. Buckwheat noodles, used in many of the recipes here, cook in only 6–8 minutes and are also delicious cold in a packed lunch the next day.

NUTS & SEEDS

These can often be used interchangeably in the recipes – you certainly don't need all of the varieties listed below; just try sesame seeds, walnuts, pumpkin seeds and cashews to begin with. Choose raw nuts/seeds and avoid ready-roasted and salted. If you consume lots of nuts and seeds day to day, ideally soak them when you can (p. 277). Toasting nuts and seeds really brings out their flavour and gives an extra crunch. Simply pop in a wide dry pan and cook on a medium heat for a minute or so, tossing occasionally and keeping an eye on them to ensure they don't burn.

Nuts: Try almonds (whole, flaked and ground), cashews, macadamia nuts, pistachios, Brazil nuts.
Coconut flakes (technically not a nut)
Peanuts (technically a legume)
Seeds: Try pumpkin seeds, chia, sunflower seeds, sesame (black and white), flaxseeds.

NATURAL SWEETENERS & DRIED FRUIT (USE IN SMALL AMOUNTS)

Raw honey: Use to sweeten dressings and uncooked/raw dishes.
Maple syrup: Choose the 100% pure variety.
Dried fruit: Try dates (Medjool are the tastiest), goji berries, apricots, raisins, cranberries.

SPICES

The following spices are favourites of mine that crop up throughout the recipes and are well worth stocking up on. When it comes to chilli, bear in mind that all chilli peppers, dried or fresh, vary in strength. Thai and bird's eye chillies are hotter, for instance, and jalapeño peppers tend to be milder. Among the different kinds of chilli flakes, Aleppo pepper and *pul biber* are milder. As a general rule, it's best to start with less chilli in a dish and gradually add more. I sprinkle it liberally on many savoury dishes, but feel free to add as much or as little as you like. For more on different chilli options, see Kitchen Swaps on p. 268.

Cayenne pepper (see the note on chilli above)
Chilli powder/flakes (including chipotle, Korean, Aleppo pepper, Turkish *pul biber* – see above)
Chinese five-spice
Paprika (smoked – sweet, medium or hot)
Cinnamon (ground)
Coriander (ground)
Cumin (ground)
Cardamom (whole or ground)
Fennel seeds
Curry powder (mild, medium or hot)
Garam masala (Indian spice mix)
Ginger (ground and fresh root)
Mustard seeds
Turmeric (ground and fresh root)
Harissa (Middle Eastern spice mix: powder and paste – or make your own, p. 98)
Za'atar (Middle Eastern spice mix)

HERBS

Fresh and dried herbs can be used interchangeably in the recipes, depending on what you have to hand. One tablespoon of a chopped fresh herb can be swapped for a teaspoon of the dried herb.

Fresh: I use lots of fresh herbs in my cooking, especially parsley, basil, coriander and mint, and I love rosemary, sage, thyme and oregano. As you'll see in the recipes, I never waste the stalks of parsley, basil or coriander but chop them up finely to include in the dish. Mint stalks can be used to make tea.
Dried: If you are just getting started, go for a dried herb mix, such as 'mixed herbs' or 'Italian herbs' or 'herbes de Provence', otherwise stock up on rosemary, thyme, oregano and sage.
Bay leaves (fresh or dried)
Lemongrass (I stock up on it when I can find it fresh and freeze it)

FRIDGE & FREEZER

My fridge and freezer are better organised than my wardrobe! I'm a big fan of meal planning and having a fairly good idea of what I'm going to eat during the week ahead, which means that I don't have to shop more than once a week and so I end up saving money and time. Meal planning also means that you can get ahead and cook in batches, making full use of the fridge and freezer for storing meals, cooked basics (pp. 271) and useful leftovers. On average, I cook from scratch about three times for the entire week. On extra-busy weeks I don't cook at all and the freezer becomes my best friend! Use the following as a checklist for keeping your fridge and freezer stocked to help you save time.

Fridge

Greens and most vegetables
Meat and fish: Keep them in a bottom shelf or drawer.
Butter: I keep an unsalted for baking and cooking and a salted for spreading on my toast.
Milk: Go for full-fat, unsweetened, additive-free brands of dairy, coconut or nut/seed milk. (See also p. 276 for making your own nut/seed milk.)
Yoghurt: Buy natural, full-fat yoghurt – cow's, sheep, goat's or coconut.
Cheese: Cheese (cow's, sheep or goat's) gives an incredible boost of intense flavour. My favourites are feta, Parmesan, mature Cheddar and halloumi.
Condiments: Once opened, jars of flavour enhancers (see the list on p. 260) are best kept in the fridge.
Fermented foods: Fermented cabbage-based foods such as sauerkraut and kimchi are both delicious and good for digestion, so keep a raw 'live' variety in your fridge for adding to some of your meals. Look for the best-quality brands and make sure they are sugar- and additive-free. See also the Quickly Pickled Veg on p. 199.

Freezer

I see the freezer almost as part of the family – an extra pair of hands that pitches in to make my life so much easier. Use the following as a checklist to keep your fridge and freezer well stocked. This will save both shopping and cooking time and make cooking (and eating!) at home more enjoyable and relaxing.

MAKING THE MOST OF YOUR FREEZER
Label: Add labels with dates to remind you to eat foods within the recommended guidelines, which is between three and six months for cooked foods.
Portion up: Make a large amount and freeze in portions, individual or to feed more, to suit your needs.
Cool down: Make sure any cooked food has cooled down fully before freezing.
Don't refreeze: You can freeze freshly cooked dishes that use raw ingredients that were frozen, but don't refreeze food, raw or cooked, once it has been defrosted.

Organise your drawers: Make life easier by dedicating the drawers in your freezer to particular ingredients, e.g. one drawer for ice, vodka, berries and sliced bananas, one for greens and cooked legumes, another for ready-made items and another for raw meat and fish.

Containers: Whenever you can, avoid aluminium foil and plastic and store foods in BPA-free containers (p. 267).

BEST FOODS FOR FREEZING
I always fill the freezer with foods when they're on offer and abundant. While most can be frozen (see below), try to avoid freezing peppers, avocados and vegetables with a high water content, such as celery, cucumber, radishes and salad greens. Avoid freezing fresh herbs, too, unless you blend them up first with olive oil.

RAW FOOD
Meat and fish: If you can't always get to a good butcher or fishmonger, go when you can and buy in bulk. Freeze bones and chicken carcasses for making stock/bone broth (p. 278). Don't cook meat or fish from frozen but allow to defrost completely first. Always ensure that food is hot all the way through before serving.
Leafy greens: Spinach, kale, spring greens, chard.
Other green vegetables: Green beans, peas, broad beans, broccoli florets.
Fruits: Berries, sliced bananas.
Fresh ginger & spices: Fresh ginger, turmeric, lemongrass, curry leaves, kaffir leaves. Freeze knobs of fresh ginger or turmeric whole and grate straight from frozen.
Herb blends: Any leftover herbs or rocket/watercress can be whizzed up into a pesto (p. 67), or just blitzed with a spoonful of extra-virgin olive oil and then frozen, ready to stir into soups or stews.
Leftover coconut milk: Freeze in an ice-cube tray and add to smoothies or soups.

PREPARED FOOD
Quinoa bread: Make Quick Quinoa Bread (p. 21) in batches and slice up before freezing. (Slices can be toasted straight from frozen).
Vegetable rice: Make cauliflower, broccoli or other vegetable 'rice' (p. 272) in big batches in a food processor and freeze in portions that you can then pop straight into the pan to cook, making sure any excess liquid cooks off.
Vegetable mash: See p. 274 for how to make this. Reheat, covered, in a pan with a splash of water.
Legumes and quinoa: Cook up big batches of beans/lentils and quinoa/buckwheat from scratch and freeze in portions. They can be added to soups and stews straight from frozen.
Curry paste: Make extra and freeze it, so that you don't have to whizz a paste up each time you make a curry. See Thai Green Vegetable Curry (p. 143), Malaysian Noodle Soup (p. 68) and Keralan Turmeric Fish Curry (p. 120).
Sauces, soups & stews: Make extra and freeze them. Defrost overnight or while you're at work. If you get caught short, run the container under hot water to loosen the frozen food, then pop into a pan with a splash of water and heat through on a medium heat with a lid on. After a few minutes you may be able to break the mixture up a bit, and then you can turn up the heat, adding a little water if it's dry.
Burgers & fritters: Make extra and freeze them, ready to pop into the oven straight from frozen.
Wraps, naans & sponge cakes: These all freeze well.
Stock/bone broth: Freeze in small portions, such as in ice-cube trays, for adding straight to the pan.
Burgers & fritters: Make extra and freeze them, ready to pop into the oven straight from frozen.
Wraps, naans & sponge cakes: These all freeze well.
Stock/bone broth: Freeze in small portions, such as in ice-cube trays, for adding straight to the pan.

EQUIPMENT

Everyday essentials

You've probably got most of these already. Just make sure they're working well and that everything is easy to grab, so that cooking is more of a pleasure than a chore!

SHARP KNIFE
A good-quality, medium-to-large knife. Keep it sharp for effortless and safe chopping.

FOOD PROCESSOR
With a grating attachment – ideal for shredding vegetables for slaws and salads and chopping onions and garlic as well as for general mixing and blending of pestos, dips and curry pastes.

BLENDER
A free-standing, high-powered blender is ideal if you aim to cook regularly and make speedy dips and smoothies. A hand-held stick blender is very useful, too, especially for blitzing soups.

CHOPPING BOARD
A good-sized chopping board is very helpful, but not so big that it's a pain to wash.

BOX GRATER
Perfect for grating cheese and vegetables by hand.

FRYING PAN
A wide and deep frying pan (30cm in diameter) with a lid is the perfect piece of equipment for most of the hob-cooking in this book, as having a large surface area really speeds up the cooking. Go for a non-stick, non-toxic brand.

SAUCEPAN
A wide and deep saucepan (2–3 litres in capacity) with a lid is essential for soups, stews and porridge.

BAKING TRAY
A very large, wide baking tray or roasting tin – or two standard-sized baking trays – ideally quite deep too, is perfect for roasting vegetables and meat and for baking cookies, etc.

WOODEN SPATULAS OR SPOONS
Invest in two wooden spatulas/spoons; label one handle for savoury and the other for sweet to avoid transferring garlic and other flavours in your baking.

KITCHEN SCALES
Digital ones are preferable as they take up less space and are easier to read at a glance.

MEASURING SPOONS
Ideal for accurate tablespoon and teaspoon measures for baking.

LARGE BOWL
Great for whisking up dressings and tossing salads easily. Either use a ceramic one that doubles up as a serving bowl or invest in a light metal one.

Useful extras

Here are a few extra bits of equipment that I recommend buying, if you can, as they will help save time in the kitchen.

BAKING TINS
If you enjoy baking, invest in a 20cm square baking tin and two 20cm round sandwich tins.

LOAF TIN
Use an 8cm x 18cm loaf tin for making the Quinoa Bread (p. 21).

MUFFIN TIN
It's quicker to bake muffins than cakes or loaves and so for speedy baking a 12-hole muffin tin comes in very handy. If you don't have paper cases, simply grease the holes and divide the batter among them rather than using a standard cake tin.

FINE-MESH SIEVE
Use to double up as a colander.

SPIRALIZER
Handy if you're not a fast chopper for making noodles from vegetables for salads and stir-fries, but if you haven't got one, use a julienne peeler or regular vegetable peeler instead (p. 273).

MICROPLANE
Perfect for finely grating Parmesan, garlic, ginger, chocolate and citrus zest.

BAKING PARCHMENT
Use for lining baking tins and trays or for cooking Fish en Papillote (p. 122).

ROLLING PIN
Use for crushing nuts and chocolate as well as rolling out dough, like the crackers on p.212.

TONGS
Useful for turning baked/roasted food on a baking tray and for flipping steaks or fish over in a pan when frying on the hob.

Storing food & drink

If you've invested in a few good-quality containers, you're much more likely to pack something 'to go', enjoying good homemade food and saving money as well, instead of having to rely on buying lunch near your workplace. I recommend not using plastic containers, if you can, in order to avoid potential leakage of chemicals into food. There are brilliant brands out there that specialise in safe food storage at affordable prices, selling products that are much more stylish than they used to be!

AIRTIGHT CONTAINERS
Use for packed lunches (for salads, wraps, sandwiches and snacks) and for storing food in the fridge and freezer. Stainless-steel containers are one of the best options here as they are light to carry around. Glass lunchboxes are great, too, though less portable as they are heavier. Save screw-top glass jars and use in the fridge for storing dips, dressings and sauces. Before using, sterilise empty jars in the dishwasher or wash by hand and place in the oven to dry out for ten minutes on a low heat.

INSULATED FLASK
Use an insulated flask (500ml) for storing hot meals (soups, stews and porridge); you can fill them up in the morning and most will keep hot for a good 6 hours.

DRINKS CANTEEN
Keep a drinks canteen (500ml–1 litre) for juices, smoothies and water.

WATER FILTER
I recommend investing in a good-quality water filter. These range in price, but a basic filter is not expensive.

KITCHEN SWAPS & SAVES

If you find yourself without an ingredient, or in the throes of a mini kitchen nightmare, don't worry! It happens to all of us and most things can be resolved. Here are a few quick tips that may help you, don't be afraid to make substitutions and get creative!

Kitchen swaps

IF YOU NEED . . .	SWAP WITH . . .
1 x 400g tin of chopped tomatoes	2 tablespoons tomato purée + 400ml water 250g chopped fresh tomatoes + 150ml water
1 tablespoon chopped fresh herbs	1 teaspoon dried herbs
1 chopped fresh chilli (not Bird's Eye)	1–2 teaspoons chilli flakes ¼ teaspoon chilli powder ¼ teaspoon cayenne pepper
1 tablespoon grated fresh ginger or turmeric	¾ teaspoon ground ginger or turmeric
1 lemongrass stalk	Grated zest of 1 lemon or lime
1 tablespoon apple cider vinegar	1½ tablespoons lime or lemon juice
240g tinned (cooked) beans or lentils	100g dried beans or lentils, soaked, cooked

Kitchen saves

Here's a mini troubleshooting guide if something goes a bit wrong in the kitchen (and, let's be honest, it happens to all of us!).

SOGGY?

If your quinoa or veg mash is soggy, with visible excess water, then drain it and simmer, with the lid off the pan, for a few minutes for any moisture to evaporate

TOO THIN?

If a sauce or soup is too thin, simmer with the lid off the pan to let it reduce.

TOO THICK?

If a cooked sauce or soup is too thick, add a few heaped tablespoons of water or stock/bone broth (whatever liquid has been used in the recipe). If a dressing or pesto is too thick, add a little water, or more olive oil/lemon juice, if that's in the recipe. You might then need to adjust the seasoning.

A BIT BLAND?

If a sauce/stew tastes a bit bland (which shouldn't happen with these recipes!), try a dash of apple cider vinegar or a squeeze of lemon juice or sprinkling of lemon zest to brighten it up. If it's not salty enough, add a little sea salt or try a dash of tamari or fish sauce. If it needs a bit more kick, add a little mustard, horseradish, chilli or more black pepper.

TOO SPICY/SALTY?

Add more substance to the dish, e.g. coconut milk or cooked beans/quinoa. For a dressing or sauce, blend in some fresh avocado, nut butter or yoghurt.

BURNT?

If you burn something in a pan, e.g. onions and garlic, then just throw them out – there's no saving them. For a larger dish, e.g. a soup or dahl, resist the urge to scrape; just pour most of the dish into another pan, leaving the burnt layer and the section of the dish just above that, and soak the pan well before cleaning.

LEFTOVERS AND MAKING SOMETHING OUT OF NOTHING

Good food should never go to waste, especially when it's still fresh and perfectly usable. My Filipino Catholic Mum and army Dad, both sticklers for zero waste, had a saying: 'Every grain of rice!' Don't waste a thing, in other words. When you're down to that last handful of salad leaves, a quarter of an avocado or a few wilting herbs, think again before you throw them away. Here are a few suggestions for creating something out of seemingly nothing and saving money in the process so that you can deservedly feel pleased with yourself!

FRUIT
Berries: Simmer in a pan to make a compote and use to top yoghurt, porridge or pancakes (p. 18 and 36). Freeze fresh raspberries, blackberries and blueberries to use in desserts and smoothies.
Bananas: Cut ripe bananas and freeze to make smoothies and ice cream (p. 253 and 231).
Apples/pears and stone fruit: Stew or roast (p. 239) and use in crumble or porridge (p. 18).
Tropical fruit: Freeze pineapples and mangos in chunks for making smoothies.

LEMON OR LIME WEDGES
Squeeze any leftover lemon or lime wedges into a jug of water, or use for a smoothie, to brighten up a soup or stew or to make Tahini Lemon Drizzle (p. 146).

SALAD LEAVES AND HERBS
Watercress/rocket and fresh herbs: Blend into a Pesto (p. 67), or whizz up with a little extra-virgin olive oil, and use to top soups, stews or roast veg.
Lettuce: Grill it or fry it Asian-style.
Spinach: Blend into a smoothie or a Pesto (p. 67) or stir into a stew or dhal (p. 51).

RAW VEGETABLES
Avocado: Add to a smoothie, make guacamole (p. 53), blend into a dip or into a dressing to make it really creamy. Chop up to top a stew or soup.
Cucumber: Pickle it (p. 199), add to a smoothie or stir-fry (try it!).
Courgette: Grate into scrambled eggs or smoked trout muffins (p. 25) or slice to top a pizza (p. 153).

Broccoli/cauliflower: Save the stalks! Cut off any really knobbly bits, then thinly slice and cook with the florets, or grate when making Vegetable Rice (p. 272).

COOKED VEGETABLES
Packed brunch/lunch: Add to a Waste Not Want Now Bowl (p. 271).
Instant soup: Use to make a really quick soup: fry onions and/or garlic, add the leftover vegetables, some stock, salt and pepper, plus any herbs and spices, and blend together.
Pizza: Top a pizza (p. 153) or Pizza Omelette (p. 26).

COOKED LEGUMES
Freezer: Make a big batch and freeze them (p. 271).
Packed brunch/lunch: Fry them in spices and add to a Waste Not, Want Not Bowl (p. 72).
Dip: Add to dips, e.g. hummus or tapenade (p. 213 and 215).
Soup: Blend into soup for extra creaminess.
Baked beans/bean mash: Use for baked beans (p. 35) or to make mash (p. 198).

LIQUIDS
Coconut milk: Add to a smoothie, soup or curry, or for creamy drinks.
Nut milk: Add to a soup or for making smoothies and other drinks (pp. 252).
Tinned tomatoes: Simmer with some herbs or spices until thickened, then scramble in some eggs. To ensure you use every last drop in the tin, rinse it out with a little of whatever liquid you are using in a recipe (e.g. stock or water) and add to the dish while it is cooking.

BASICS

Here are some basic 'How Tos'. If you're not yet familiar with any of these recipes, have a read through; they are all very simple and once you've tried them for the first time, you'll have mastered them. They include three ways to enjoy more vegetables as side dishes, how to cook your own beans/lentils, and how make your own stock/bone broth and nut/seed milk and butter (if you prefer homemade to shop bought).

Beans & lentils

Tinned legumes are used throughout these recipes and they are perfect for speedy meals. When you have time, buy a big bag of your favourite type of dried beans or lentils, give them a soak (p. 277) and then cook and freeze them in separate small portions. It will save you money and nothing beats the texture of home-cooked beans. Buy from a good supplier with a high turnover, as old beans will take forever to cook. After you've soaked the beans/lentils, here's how to cook them. Always refer to the packet, too, for cooking times.

● Tip

Cooking times: Lentils and mung beans take 25–40 minutes. Chickpeas take 1½–2 hours and all other beans take between 50 minutes and 1¼ hours.

Raw/cooked weights: 200g dried beans/lentils = 500g cooked beans/lentils = 2 x 400g tins of cooked beans/lentils (480g drained weight).

1. Rinse the beans/lentils well before and after soaking. Place the soaked beans/lentils in a large pan and cover with about three times the volume of water.

2. Bring to the boil, then reduce to a low simmer and skim off any foam that rises to the surface during cooking.

3. Place the lid on, cook until tender (see tips and check the packet instructions) but not mushy – taste one or two to be sure – then drain and allow to cool before serving or freezing.

Vegetable rice

You can easily make vegetable 'rice', either by hand, with a box grater, or with a food processor. I really recommend the food processor, especially if cooking for four people or more, as it's much quicker and easier. You can also make double or triple batches and put them straight into the freezer to have some already grated for another time. Serve the rice plain, or mix and match with your choice of fresh or dried herbs and spices and other flavourings to make it the star of the show.

Serves 4 as a side

2 teaspoons butter, coconut
  oil or ghee
Sea salt and black pepper
1 handful of dried fruit, seeds,
  chopped (toasted) nuts or
  coconut flakes, to serve
  (optional)

VEGETABLE OPTIONS
1 large cauliflower (900g),
  outer leaves removed
2 heads of broccoli (total 800g)
3 large carrots
2 large sweet potatoes, peeled
1 small squash, peeled
  and deseeded

OPTIONAL EXTRAS
1 handful of chopped spring
  onions, onion, leek or chives
1 garlic clove, finely chopped
1 tablespoon chopped fresh
  herbs (mint, coriander, basil
  or dill) or 1 teaspoon dried
  herbs (rosemary, thyme,
  oregano or za'atar)
1 teaspoon ground spices
  (harissa, garam masala,
  ginger or chilli)

SEASONING OPTIONS
A squeeze of lemon or
  lime juice
A dash of tamari, toasted
  sesame oil or fish sauce

1. Melt the butter in a wide frying pan over a medium heat. Add any optional extras, followed by your choice of grated vegetable, and stir-fry for 30 seconds. Add 2–6 tablespoons of water (you'll need less for the cauliflower/broccoli and more for the root vegetables/squash), put a lid on the pan and steam for 3–4 minutes (for cauliflower/broccoli) or 8 minutes (for root vegetables/squash). Alternatively you can stir-fry the 'rice', cooking for about the same length of time and strring every now and then. Add a splash of water to the pan, if you need to.

2. Season to taste or add your choice of seasoning. For abit of extra texture stir in some dried fruit or seeds/chopped nuts to serve, if you like.

Using a grater:
Use the coarse side of the grater to grate your choice of vegetable. If using cauliflower or broccoli, use the stalk as a 'handle' to hold the cauliflower/broccoli while you grate it into rice-sized pieces. Make sure to grate everything, including the stalk.

Using a food processor:
Select either the S-curved blade or the grater attachment and use a sharp knife to chop your choice of vegetable into chunks – ones that are small enough to fit into the feed tube if using the grater attachment. (Make sure to include the stalk for cauliflower/broccoli.) Add your choice of vegetable to the food processor and pulse for about 20 seconds.

Vegetable noodles

Making vegetable noodles with a spiralizer is super-quick, but a julienne peeler or standard vegetable peeler works just as well. You just need to apply a bit more pressure when peeling, to make thick, wide noodles. With a spiralizer you can turn most vegetables (courgettes, cucumbers, celeriac, swede, squash, beetroot, sweet potatoes, large carrots and even apples) into noodle shapes, but it's also brilliant if you don't like chopping, as it makes short work of slicing onions, peppers or cabbages – perfect for a stir-fry. For recipes that use vegetable noodles, have a look at the Pad Thai Noodles (p. 136) or the Sesame Carrot & Courgette Noodle Salad/Stir-fry (p. 164). To make them into a light salad, add a dressing such as the Ginger Tahini Dressing (p.146) or toss with Pesto (p. 67).

Serves 4 as a side

500g courgettes, cucumbers, beetroots or large carrots

Spiralizer: Slice the ends off your choice of vegetable to get straight lines and then spiralize. Use scissors or a knife to cut long strands into shorter lengths to makes them easier to eat.

Julienne or standard vegetable peeler: Peel your choice of vegetable into wide strips, which you can serve like this or slice each wide strip lengthways in half or into thirds to create thinner strands.

RAW OR STIR-FRIED
Courgettes, cucumbers, carrots, beetroots

STIR-FRIED, STEAMED OR ROASTED
Celeriac, swede, squash, sweet potatoes

Vegetable mash

Whether eaten on the side or used as a topping for a casserole or pie, mash makes for a comforting meal. Vegetable mash can be made in just the same way as standard mashed potato, so play around with different vegetables and flavourings, or even combine veg, such as broccoli and pea, cauliflower and parsnip, celeriac and butternut squash. See the Veggie Cottage Pie with Cauliflower Mash (p. 149) and try the Butter Bean Mash (p. 198) served with lamb chops. Why not try roasted swede or parsnip mash with your next Sunday roast or celeriac and leek mash with sausages or a steak. Stir in spring onions, chives, horseradish, a handful of cheese or even a touch of truffle oil as an optional extra to liven them up!

Cauliflower or broccoli mash

Serves 4 as a side

1 large cauliflower or 2 heads of broccoli (about 900g), chopped into equal-sized florets
100ml water
2 garlic cloves, roughly chopped (optional)
2 tablespoons butter
Sea salt and black pepper

1. Place the florets in a wide, deep pan, add the water and the garlic (if using). Cover with a lid, then turn the heat up to medium-high and steam for 5 minutes until tender. Drain well and return to the dry pan.

2. Add the butter and mash by hand with a potato masher, then season to taste with salt and pepper. Alternatively, you could blitz everything in a food processor or high-powered blender.

Root vegetable mash

The vegetables for this mash can be cooked on the stove, like the cauliflower or broccoli, but they are also great roasted to bring out the natural sweetness. Any root vegetables would do here: choose from 1 large celeriac, or swede, 1 small squash or 4 large carrots or parsnips.

Serves 4 as a side

800g root vegetables (see above), peeled and chopped into 2cm cubes
200ml water
3 garlic cloves, roughly chopped (optional)
1 tablespoon coconut oil or ghee (if cooking in the oven)
3 tablespoons butter
Sea salt and black pepper

1. **Hob:** Place the vegetables in a wide, deep pan, add about 200ml of water and the garlic (if using). Cover with a lid, turn the heat up to medium-high and allow to steam for 10–15 minutes until tender. Drain well and return to the dry pan.

   Oven: Preheat the oven to 220°C/Gas mark 9, add the oil to a roasting tin and pop in the oven for a few minutes to melt. Toss the chopped vegetables in the melted oil and roast in the oven for 20–25 minutes until tender.

2. Add the butter and mash by hand with a potato masher, then season to taste with salt and pepper. Alternatively, you could blitz everything in a food processor or high-powered blender.

Nut/seed milk

You'll need a food processor or a high-powered blender and a nut milk bag or a muslin cloth – cheap and easy to get.

Makes about 1.25 litres milk

250g nuts or seeds
1 litre water

OPTIONAL EXTRAS
½ teaspoon ground spices (such as cinnamon, turmeric or ginger)
1 teaspoon cocoa powder
1 teaspoon vanilla extract

1. Place the nuts or seeds in a food processor or high-powered blender and pour in the water. Blitz for 30–60 seconds, depending on the strength of your blender, until the nuts/seeds have completely broken down.

2. Use a muslin cloth or nut milk bag to strain the mixture into a jug or wide-mouthed bottle. Once the mixture has gone through, squeeze the cloth really well until no more liquid comes out, then stir in any optional extras and store in a sterilised bottle (p. 267) in the fridge for up to 5 days.

Nut/seed butter

For a richer flavour, you could lightly toast the nuts/seeds first – in the oven at fan 170 °C/Gas mark 5 for 5–10 minutes, or in a dry pan on the hob for a couple of minutes – tossing occasionally and keeping your eye on them as they can easily burn!

Makes about 250g butter

250g nuts or seeds
2 teaspoons coconut oil

OPTIONAL EXTRAS
½ teaspoon ground spices (cinnamon, turmeric, ginger)
1 teaspoon cocoa powder
1 teaspoon vanilla extract

1. Add the nuts/seeds and coconut oil to a food processor with any optional extras. Blitz everything together for 1–2 minutes, then use a spatula to scrape down the sides of the processor bowl. Blitz the mixture again until smooth.

2. If you want a slightly chunky butter, blitz for 30 seconds and remove a few spoonfuls. Keep blitzing until smooth and then stir through the reserved spoonfuls. Transfer to an airtight container – a sterilised screw-top jar (p. 267) would be perfect – and keep in the fridge for up to 2 weeks.

NUT OPTIONS
Almonds, Brazils, cashews, hazelnuts, pistachios, pecans, walnuts, macadamia nuts

SEED OPTIONS
Hemp, sunflower, sesame, pumpkin seeds

Soaking nuts, seeds & beans

Soaking is especially worthwhile for anyone who eats large amounts of raw nuts, seeds, dried legumes or quinoa and buckwheat, as it helps you to digest them better and has the added benefit of shortening the cooking time. To get into the soaking habit, when you're making supper have a think about what you're cooking the next day, then soak whatever you think you'll need. It takes just a few minutes and saves you time in the end. If you don't get a chance to do any soaking, don't worry but rinse everything very well before cooking.

HOW TO SOAK

It's very simple. Just put whatever you're intending to soak in a large bowl, cover with plenty of water (allowing at least 5cm on top), add a pinch of salt and a dash of lemon juice or apple cider vinegar and leave for 2 hours for raw cashews and at least 8 hours, or overnight, for anything else. It's best to check packet instructions, too, as the time varies according to the particular ingredient. After soaking, drain and rinse really well until the water runs clear.

NO NEED TO SOAK

There's no need to soak red split lentils (which are already hulled and split), Brazil nuts, pine nuts, chia seeds, flaxseeds or ground nuts or seeds. Nor do you need to soak tinned beans, chickpeas and lentils, of course, as they are already cooked.

Homemade stock/bone broth

Made with either animal bones or vegetables, stock has been a staple in many cultures for centuries. A good meat stock, or bone broth, is made from high-quality bones that are slowly simmered in plenty of water to extract all the nutrients and flavour. Good-quality shop-bought stock is handy when time is short (see www.melissahemsley.com for recommendations), but do check the ingredients. A good stock should be made only with bones/vegetables and natural flavourings. To be sure that there are no unwanted ingredients, there is nothing like making your own from scratch. I make it a few times a month and freeze it in separate portions. Depending on the size of your pan, allow about 1kg of bones for every 1 litre of water.

Bone broth

Buy chicken carcasses, lamb or beef bones from your butcher or use a leftover chicken carcass from a Sunday roast for this. I also like to save the ends of fresh vegetables and herbs (see Vegetable Stock opposite) to flavour the broth, but they are not essential.

Makes 2–3 litres

2–3kg bones or chicken carcasses

2–3 litres water (however much liquid your biggest pan can hold)

1 tablespoon apple cider vinegar

OPTIONAL EXTRAS
Onion, leek, carrot or celery ends
1 handful of parsley stalks
A few bay leaves

1. Add all the ingredients to your largest pan (or slow cooker).

2. Put a tight-fitting lid on the pan, bring to the boil and then reduce to a very low simmer, allowing at least 12 hours for lamb or beef and 6 hours or more for chicken. Cook on the high setting for 12 hours if using a slow cooker, cooking for 12 hours for lamb/beef or 6–8 hours for chicken. Taste and adjust seasoning as required.

3. After the recommended time, strain and leave to cool before storing in the fridge (for 4–5 days) or freezer.

✳ Use it Up

If some meat is left on the bones, simmer for about 30 minutes until the meat is cooked, then remove from the pan. Pull off the meat when cool enough to handle and add the bones back to the pan to continue simmering. Two chicken carcasses will provide a bowl's worth of meat scraps to enjoy in soups or stews. You can use ice-cube trays to freeze stock/bone broth, making it easy to use in small quantities.

Vegetable stock

Use this as a basic guide for making a delicious vegetable stock to add depth to soups, risotto, stews and quinoa. You can use whole fresh vegetables for the stock or bits of vegetables left over from cooking other dishes during the week. Keep ends of vegetables with this in mind; you can freeze them if you're not planning to use them straight away and add them straight to the pan of water when you're ready to make stock. Likewise, use whatever fresh herbs you have to hand or swap with dried herbs. Just avoid any vegetables from the cruciferous family – broccoli, cabbage, kale – as the flavour will be overpowering!

Makes 2–3 litres

2–3 litres water (however much liquid your biggest pan can hold)
4 garlic cloves, roughly chopped
1 large handful of roughly chopped onions or leeks
1 large handful of roughly chopped carrots
2 celery sticks, roughly chopped
1 teaspoon sea salt
1 teaspoon black peppercorns or ½ teaspoon ground black pepper

OPTIONAL EXTRAS
1 handful of parsley stalks
1 large sprig of fresh thyme
2 bay leaves
1 tablespoon dried mixed herbs

1. Add all the ingredients to your largest pan, including any fresh or dried herbs, if using.

2. Put a tight-fitting lid on the pan, bring to the boil and then reduce to a very low simmer stirring ocassionally, allowing at least 1 hour. Taste and adjust seasoning.

3. Strain and leave to cool before storing in the fridge for up to a week or for up to 6 months in the freezer.

Thank You to...

The biggest thanks to Anna Lisle, Kitty Coles, Evangelina Hemsley for helping me perfect the recipes and being the ultimate in support and love.

My shooting dream team of Emily Ezekiel with Kitty Coles for props, art direction and styling, and Issy Croker for photography, ably assisted by Stephanie McCleod. Thanks to Liam, Adam, Issy and Louise for helping us out on the shoot days and making it so much fun.

My book family: Lizzy Gray (we now have three books together and counting!), Jessica Barnfield, Kate Parker, Rebecca Smart, Sarah Bennie, Kealey Rigden, Di Riley, Caroline Butler, Rae Shirvington, Lucy Harrison and Jake Lingwood and everyone at Ebury Press – you're the best.

To so many friends and family for recipe testing and giving EAT HAPPY a big thumbs up: Ruth and Anais Sanders, Amanda Sanchez Barry, Sarah Malcolm, Louise Rapson, Sima Bibi, Rebecca and Nick Bateman, Roxy and Will Houshmand Howell, Shelley Martin Light, Steve Ball, Chris Mason and Hannah, Alex Rose and Caroline Jackson, Jo and Lorraine Mitchell, Jasmin Harsono, Nadia Parham, Florence Lefebreve, Monica Kaiser, Liz and Aggy McCarthy, Anne Steer, the Smiths - Janet, Imogen, Richard and Maddi, Fiona Hemming, Pete Barker, Martha Whelan and Aniqah Moawalla, and Ros Heathcote.

And special thank you to Henry, for (spontaneously) shooting the front cover of EAT HAPPY, for restoring a house and building me a dream kitchen so I could dedicate my time to writing this book. (Oh and for all the washing up!) To Nelly, taking big long walks with you gives me all the inspiration I need.

To Mum, this book is for you, for making me 'brain snacks' for school, for teaching me to never waste food, and for being my biggest and kindest helper, always.

Melissa Hemsley celebrates quick and easy healthy food that everyone can enjoy.
Melissa is one of the sisters in Hemsley + Hemsley, the bestselling authors of
The Art of Eating Well and *Good + Simple* with their own cafe at Selfridges, London.

@melissa.hemsley   @hemsleyhemsley

@melissahemsley   hemsleyandhemsley.com

@melissahemsleycooks

melissahemsley.com

1 3 5 7 9 10 8 6 4 2

Ebury Press, an imprint of Ebury Publishing,
20 Vauxhall Bridge Road,
London, SW1V 2SA

Ebury Press is part of the Penguin Random House group of companies whose addresses
can be found at global.penguinrandomhouse.com

Copyright © Melissa Hemsley 2018
Photography © Issy Croker 2018

Melissa Hemsley has asserted her right to be identified as the author of
this Work in accordance with the Copyright, Designs and Patents Act 1988

First published by Ebury Press in 2018
www.penguin.co.uk

A CIP catalogue record for this book is available from the British Library

Design: Two Associates
Photography: Issy Croker, except p. 4, 195 Henry Ralph and p. 288 Ellie Dunbar
Cover Photo: Henry Ralph

ISBN 9781785036637

Colour reproduction by Altaimage Ltd
Printed and bound in Germany by Firmengruppe APPL, aprinta druck, Wemding

Penguin Random House is committed to a sustainable future for our business, our readers
andour planet. This book is made from Forest Stewardship Council® certified paper.